THE CHRIST OF THE EMPTY TOMB

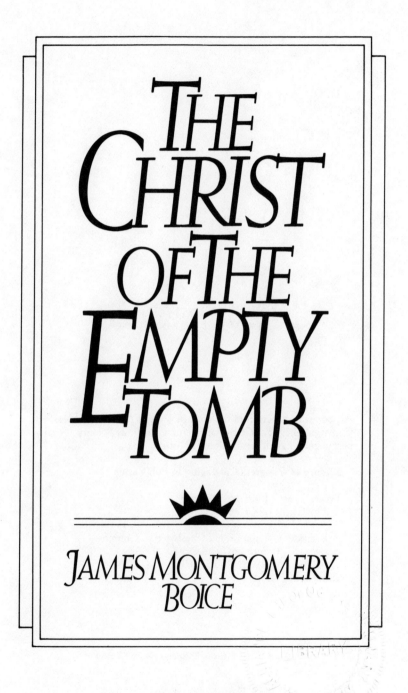

THE CHRIST OF THE EMPTY TOMB

JAMES MONTGOMERY BOICE

MOODY PRESS

CHICAGO

All Scripture taken from the *Holy Bible: New International Version.*
Copyright © 1973, 1978 by the International Bible Society. Used by
permission of Zondervan Bible Publishers.

Library of Congress Cataloging in Publication Data

Boice, James Montgomery, 1938-
  The Christ of the empty tomb.

  1. Easter—Sermons.   2. Presbyterian Church—
Sermons.   3. Sermons, American.   I. Title.
BV4259.B65   1985   252'.63   84-27338
ISBN 0-8024-1303-X

1 2 3 4 5 6 7 Printing/RR/Year 89 88 87 86 85

Printed in the United States of America

To Him
who has swallowed up death
in victory

Contents

Preface

As I write this, a little more than seven months has passed since the appearance of a volume of Christmas messages entitled *The Christ of Christmas*. That volume appeared prior to Christmas 1983 and was intended for the holiday trade. It was not expected to sell a great many copies. So Moody Press and I were somewhat surprised when the fairly large first printing immediately sold out and it became impossible to get additional copies even six weeks before Christmas.

This unusual response to that book encouraged me to think that there might be similar interest in a companion book of Easter messages. Like the first, this book is a collection of sermons preached at Tenth Presbyterian Church over a span of years stretching from approximately 1969 to 1982. Most of the sermons were preached on Easter Sunday, and most were also aired (usually one year later) over the international radio program "The Bible Study Hour," on which I was the speaker for that same period of time. Occasionally I preached these messages in other places too. Some of the material has appeared in slightly altered form in early books of mine.

In pulling these diverse messages together for inclusion in this volume I have been struck again with two things.

First, the resurrection was totally unexpected by those who first saw the Lord. He had told them about it, of course. He had prophesied: "The Son of Man will be betrayed to the chief priests and teachers of the law. They will condemn him to death and will hand him over to the Gentiles, who will mock him and spit on him, flog him and kill him. Three days later he will rise" (Mark 10:33-34). This and other prophecies are so explicit that we can hardly understand how the disciples failed to grasp Christ's teaching and expect the resurrection, especially since Christ's enemies seem to have understood His claim although they disbelieved it.

But so it was! Cleopas and Mary, the Emmaus disciples, heard reports of the resurrection but had so little interest in them that they simply went on packing for their trip home following the Sabbath. Mary Magdalene could think only of Christ's body. Thomas, the most outspoken, said, "Unless I see the nail marks in his hands and put my finger where the nails were, and put my hand into his side, I will not believe it" (John 20:25). They were not gullible men and women, as some have pictured them to be. They were hard-nosed skeptics. They were as resistant to miracles as our contemporaries.

Second, I have been impressed with how utterly convinced the disciples became once they had seen the glorified Jesus. And it was not just a matter of one or two having claimed to have seen Him. All the disciples, all the women— indeed even five hundred people at one time—saw Jesus, and this was so overwhelming to them that not once after that did any one of them ever question the miracle. Many times they sinned. They had fallings out among themselves. They erred in other things. But never once did any doubt that Jesus really was raised from the dead and that His resurrection proved all that needs to be proved for Christianity. It proved:

That there is a God and that the God of the Bible is the true God;
That Jesus is God's unique Son and that He is fully divine;
That all who believe in Jesus Christ are justified from all sin;
That the believer in Christ can have supernatural victory over sin in this life; and
That we too shall rise again.

It is for these reasons that the resurrection of Jesus Christ is good news. In fact, it is the best news the world has ever heard. It is news that needs to be proclaimed vigorously and joyously to our own sinful and dying generation.

The congregation of Tenth Presbyterian graciously supports me in this and many other writing projects, and I am thankful for their encouragement in this important aspect of my ministry. They also join me in praying that these studies, first preached to them, might now equally be blessed as they are commended to a wider, reading audience. As always, I wish to thank my faithful secretary, Caecilie M. Foelster, for her careful typing (and retyping) of the manuscript and for her care in checking references and other details.

"Thanks be to God! He gives us the victory through our Lord Jesus Christ" (1 Corinthians 15:57).

1. *He Lives!*

I do not know if you have had the experience of gaining an insight or receiving a revelation so important that you wished it could be preserved forever. If you have, or if you have even experienced that in a partial way, you will understand the tone in which Job spoke his most widely quoted lines, beginning, "I know that my Redeemer lives." We hear something said in a particularly vivid way, and we say, "If I could just remember that!" Or we have an insight and say, "If I could just get that written down so I won't forget it!"

That was the feeling that Job experienced. He had suffered a great deal, first by the loss of his possessions, then by the loss of his ten children and eventually his own health. His friends came to comfort but actually abused him, charging that his misfortunes were the result of some particularly outstanding sin in his life. In the midst of one reply Job gave vent to the insight to which I am referring.

Job perceived that his story was not being told completely in this life and that a later day would vindicate him. In fact, he perceived that there was an *individual* who would vindicate him, even Jesus Christ, whom Job calls "my Redeemer." This individual would stand on the earth in some future day, would raise Job from death, and would enable him to see God.

Can you imagine Job's excitement as he gave expression to this hope? There were not many who shared it in Job's day; few understood it. So Job said that he wished his words might be preserved. "Oh, that my words were recorded, that they were written on a scroll, that they were inscribed with an iron tool on lead, or engraved in rock forever!" (Job 19:23-24). Fortunately for us, Job's wish was fulfilled. Not only were his words preserved in a book; they have been preserved in the Book of books, the Bible.

A KINSMAN-REDEEMER

"I know that my Redeemer lives, and that in the end he will stand upon the earth" (19:25).

13

The first thing we shall look at in Job's statement is its key word: "Redeemer." This is a rich and particularly illuminating term. In Hebrew the word is *goel,* which refers to a relative who performs the office of a redeemer for his kin. We must visualize a situation in which a Hebrew has lost his inheritance through debt. He has mortgaged his estate and, because of a lack of money to meet the debt, is about to lose it. This happened in the case of Naomi and Ruth so that, although they had once possessed land, they had become impoverished. In such a situation it was the *goel's* duty, as the next of kin, to buy the inheritance; that is, to pay the mortgage and restore the land to his relative. Boaz did that for Ruth.

That custom is what Job refers to in his expression of faith in a divine Redeemer, and it is why this passage must refer to Job's own resurrection. As Job spoke those words he was in dire physical condition. He had lost family and health. He must have imagined that he was about to lose his life, too. He would die. Worms would destroy his body. But that was not the end of the story. For his body, like the land, was his inheritance; and there is one who will redeem it for him. Years may go by, but at the latter day the Redeemer will stand upon earth and will perform the office of a *goel* in raising his body. He will bring Job into the presence of God.

I recognize that there are different ways of translating the phrase "Yet in my flesh I will see God" (19:26). Some versions read, "Yet without my flesh." But those fail to make full sense of the passage. What is redeemed if it is not Job's body? Not the soul or spirit certainly, for those are never forfeited. And not Job's physical possessions, for the passage is not even considering them. It is the body that will be redeemed. Consequently, it is in this body and with his own physical eyes that Job expects to see God.

A second duty of the *goel* was to redeem by power, if that should be necessary. Abraham performed this duty when Lot had been captured by the four kings who made war against the king of Sodom and his allies. Abraham armed his household, pursued the four kings and their prisoners, and then, attacking by night, recovered both prisoners and spoil. That is what the Lord Jesus Christ did, was it not? He attacked in power—we speak rightly of resurrection power—and broke death's hold.

Finally, the *goel* had a duty to avenge a death. Imagine that an Israelite has been attacked and is dying. The *goel* learns who has struck his relative. He snatches up his own sword and dashes off to avenge the murder. Our Christ is likewise our avenger. We are dying people, but we have a Redeemer. We read of Him: "For he must reign until he has put all his enemies under his feet. The last enemy to be destroyed is death. . . . Where, O death, is your victory? Where, O death, is your sting? The sting of death is sin, and the power of sin is the law. But thanks be to God! He gives us the victory through our Lord Jesus Christ" (1 Corinthians 15:25-26, 55-57).

A LIVING REDEEMER

As we think about his words in greater detail, we discover next that Job took confidence, not only in the fact that he had a Redeemer, but that he had a *living* Redeemer. That is important, because a redeemer must be living to perform his function.

If Job had been able to say merely that he had a Redeemer, that would have been wonderful. If he could have said further that the Redeemer of whom he was speaking was the Christ, that would have been even more wonderful. To have known such a one, to have been related to him, to have been able to look back to what he had done—all that would have been both pleasant and comforting. But so far as the present need was concerned it would have been inadequate. A person in that position could say, "I had a Redeemer, and I value that." But he would undoubtedly add, "But I wish I had him now." A redeemer must be living if he is to buy back the estate, recover the prisoners, and defeat the enemy.

Job does not say that he *had* a Redeemer. He says that he *has* a Redeemer and that he is *living*. We too have a living Redeemer, the same Redeemer, who is Jesus.

That is the thrust of our testimony on Easter Sunday and indeed on every other Lord's Day. We testify that Jesus rose from the dead and that he ever lives to help all who call upon him. The evidences for this are overwhelming. There is the evidence of the narratives themselves. They are quite evidently four separate and independent accounts, for if they were not, there would not be so many apparent discrepancies—the time at which the women went to the tomb, the number of the angels, and so on. At the same time, it is also obvious that there is a deep harmony among them—not a superficial harmony but rather a detailed harmony that is increasingly evident as the accounts are analyzed. In fact, the situation is precisely what we should expect if the accounts are four independent records of those who were eyewitnesses.

One writer summarized the evidence like this:

> It is plain that these accounts must be either a record of facts that actually occurred, or else fictions. If fictions, they must have been fabricated in one of two ways, either independently of one another, or in collusion with one another. They cannot have been made up independently; the agreements are too marked and too many. They cannot have been made up in collusion . . . the apparent discrepancies are too numerous and too noticeable. Not made up independently, not made up in collusion, therefore it is evident that they were not made up at all. They are a true relation of facts as they actually occurred.[1]

The resurrection of the Lord Jesus Christ is also proved by the transformed lives of the disciples. Before the resurrection two negative charges could be made

---

1. R. A. Torrey, *The Bible and Its Christ: Being Noonday Talks with Business Men on Faith and Unbelief* (New York: Revell, 1904-1906), pp. 60-61.

against them; and these by their own confession. First, they had failed to understand Jesus' teaching about His crucifixion and resurrection. Second, they were cowardly. Peter had said that he would defend Jesus to the death and that he would never deny him. But on the night of the arrest he did deny Him. He abandoned Him, as did the other disciples. On the day of the resurrection, but before Jesus had appeared to them in the upper room, we find them hiding for fear of the Jews. Yet hours later they were standing up boldly in Jerusalem to denounce the execution of Jesus and call for faith in Him. Moreover, when they were arrested later we do not find them cowering in fear of the future but rather giving full testimony to Christian faith and doctrine. What made the difference? What made cowards bold, a scattering body of individuals a cohesive force, a disillusioned following evangelists? Only one thing accounts for it: the resurrection of Jesus Christ.

There are many evidences, but I cannot help but mention a third—the change in the day of worship. Before the resurrection the followers of Christ worshiped, as did all Jews, on Saturday. The need to do this would not even have been questioned—it had been practiced for centuries. Yet from that time on we find the newly formed body of Christians meeting, not on Saturday, but on the first day of the week, Sunday. Clearly it was because of Jesus' resurrection.

A Personal Redeemer

There is a third point to Job's statement. Not only does Job declare that he has a Redeemer, not only does he affirm that He is a living Redeemer—he adds, quite properly, that He is *his* Redeemer. "My" is the word he uses. "I know that *my* Redeemer lives." Do you know that "my" in relation to Jesus Christ? It is a reminder of the need for personal religion.

This is what we desire, is it not? We are persons, and we desire personal relationships. We are made in God's image, as persons; so we desire a personal relationship with God.

In my church I notice that the young people often have a great deal of appreciation for one another. There are young women, for instance, who greatly appreciate certain young men. And there are young men who greatly appreciate certain young women, even though they sometimes fail to say so. That is a wonderful thing. I am glad that virtue and good looks are noticed. But I have observed that in addition there are also many young women who would like to be able to say, not only, "Look at that fellow; how handsome he is!" but also, "Look at *my* fellow." And some of the young men would like to say, "Look at *my* girl," Admiration is good, but personal involvement is better.

That is our privilege in relation to Christ. It is good to admire Him. He is the risen Lord of glory after all; it would be foolish not to do so. But how much better to know Him personally, as Job did. Jesus came to earth to die for sin and to rise again. Can you say, "My God came as *my* Redeemer to die for *my* sin and to rise again for *my* justification"? You give no real evidence of being a Christian until you can.

Do not delay. Do not say, "I'll do it next year." I can give no guarantee that you will be here next year. On the contrary, *some* who read these words will not be. Even tomorrow may be too late. The Bible says, "Now is the time of God's favor, now is the day of salvation" (2 Corinthians 6:2).

ASSURANCE

I would also like you to possess Job's assurance. That is the fourth point. Not only does Job refer to his Redeemer and declare that he is both a living and personal Redeemer, he also says that he knows these things: "I know that my Redeemer lives, and that in the end he will stand upon the earth." You should possess such assurance if you are a Christian.

I do not know why some people think that it is meritorious to express doubt in matters of religion. They think that it is somehow vain or impolite to be certain and that it is humble and therefore desirable to say, "I do not know. . . . I hope so. . . . I would like to believe. . . . I think. . . . " Nothing could be more faulty. The humble person is the one who bows before God's revelation and accepts it because of who God is. It is the proud man who thinks he knows enough about anything to doubt God. Besides, God says that doubt is the equivalent of calling Him a liar; it is as much as to say that His word is untrustworthy (cf. 1 John 5:10).

Jesus lives! Believe it! Declare it! Act upon it! Say with Job, "I know that my Redeemer lives," and realize that certain important benefits flow from it.

What are those benefits? We have already alluded to them. The most obvious is that believers in Jesus Christ will live again. Job refers to that by adding, "After my skin has been destroyed, yet in my flesh I will see God" (v. 26). Because our Redeemer lives, we shall live. His resurrection is the pledge of our own.

Then, too, we shall see God. That is the second benefit. We shall live again and in that living form shall see God. What a wonderful thought. And how much more wonderful than anything else that might be said. Notice that Job does not say, "I shall see heaven." That was true, but it was relatively unimportant compared to the fact that he would see God. Spurgeon wrote, "He does not say, 'I shall see the pearly gates, I shall see the walls of jasper, I shall see the crowns of gold and the harps of harmony,' but 'I shall see God'; as if that were the sum and substance of heaven."[2] Nor does he say, "I shall see the holy angels." That would have been a magnificent sight, at least it seems so to us as we look through the eyes of John the evangelist, who wrote the book of Revelation. I find few scenes more thrilling than John's description. But that too pales beside the gaze of the soul on God. Notice, finally, that Job did not even say, "I shall see those of this world who

---

2. Charles Haddon Spurgeon, "I Know that My Redeemer Liveth," in *Metropolitan Tabernacle Pulpit*, vol. 9 (Pasadena, Tex.: Pilgrim Publications, 1969), p. 214.

have gone to heaven before me," even though that would be a great joy and his departed children would be among them. Job would see all these things: the pearly gates, the holy angels, his children. But over and above and infinitely more glorious than any of those, he would see God.

Do not think that this is a narrow vista, wonderful but small, like looking at one of those old-fashioned pastoral scenes within a candy egg. God is infinite. To see God is to experience perfect contentment and to be satisfied in all one's faculties.

LIVING MEMORIALS

Our conclusion is this: If Job, who lived at the dawn of recorded history, centuries before the time of the Lord Jesus Christ—if Job knew these things, how much more should we know them, we who are aware of Christ's resurrection and have witnessed His power in our lives. Job lived in a dark and misty time, before the dawning of the Lord Jesus Christ, that sun of righteousness. Job lived in an age before Jesus brought life and immortality to light through the gospel. If he had failed to understand about the resurrection and had failed to believe in it, who could blame him? Nobody. Yet he believed. How much more then should we?

Can you say with Job, "I know that my Redeemer lives, and that in the end he will stand upon the earth. And after my skin has been destroyed, yet in my flesh I will see God"? If so, then live in that assurance. Do not fear death. During the next twelve months death will certainly come for some, but there will also be a resurrection. Besides, Jesus is also coming; and if that should happen soon, He will receive us all.

I add one more thought. We believe these truths, yes. But let us not only believe them; let us pass them on so that others may share in this resurrection faith also. What was Job's desire after all? It was that his words might be preserved and that his faith in the resurrection might be saved for coming generations. The resurrection hope has come down to us through many centuries of church history. Let it pass to our children and to our children's children until the living Lord Jesus Christ returns in His glory. Jesus Christ lives. He lives! Then let us tell others, and let us shout with Job, "I know that my Redeemer lives, and that in the end he will stand upon the earth."

2. "I Am the Life"

During the first century B.C. a famous letter was written by Sulpicius Severus, a Roman, to Cicero, the great orator, on the occasion of the death of Cicero's beloved daughter Tullia. The letter expressed deep sympathy and reminded the orator that his daughter had only experienced the common lot of mankind and had passed away only when the freedom of the republic itself was failing. It was warm and moving, but it contained nothing of a hope of life beyond the grave. In reply, Cicero thanked his friend for his sympathy and enlarged upon the magnitude of his loss.

A century later the apostle Paul had an opportunity to write to Christians who were in a situation similar to that of Cicero. They had become discouraged by the death of a number of their friends. To them Paul said, "Brothers, we do not want you to be ignorant about those who fall asleep, or to grieve like the rest of men, who have no hope. We believe that Jesus died and rose again and so we believe that God will bring with Jesus those who have fallen asleep in him. . . . Therefore encourage each other with these words" (1 Thessalonians 4:13-14, 18).

Those letters—one from Sulpicius Severus and one from Paul—present a remarkable contrast, and they throw into sharp relief the new conception of the future life introduced by the Christian faith. Cicero was not unaware of Plato's arguments for immortality, but those were poor comfort in face of the cruel horror of death and of the irrevocable loss of one he loved. Paul spoke of hope and confidence, and his words are effective consolation to all who suffer loss. Hope, confidence, and consolation. Where did those things originate? The answer is that they were brought into the world by Jesus Christ. They are based on the truth of Jesus' resurrection and upon the reality of a personal fellowship with Him.

A NEW HOPE

In the events of John 11 that new hope was unveiled for the first time. There Jesus says, "I am the resurrection and the life. He who believes in me will live, even though he dies; and whoever lives and believes in me will never die" (vv. 25-26).

Mary, Martha, and Lazarus lived in Bethany not far from the city of Jerusalem. Jesus knew the family well. According to Luke, Jesus had visited their home on several occasions. At one time, when He was teaching, Mary had sat at His feet to learn instead of preparing a meal—to the dismay of her older sister. John indicates that Jesus made their residence his home base during the final weeks of His ministry. Presumably Jesus and His disciples set out from the home of Mary, Martha, and Lazarus each morning of His final week in Jerusalem, prior to His crucifixion, and returned there each evening at nightfall. It was on the last of those journeys, as Jesus deliberately tarried in the Garden of Gethsemane, that He was arrested. From these references it is evident that their home was one to which Jesus loved to go. He loved each member of the family, and they loved Him.

Now trouble came into that family, and Jesus was not there to help them. He had been there a few days previously but had gone away, telling them where He was going. While He was gone Lazarus became sick, and the sickness was serious enough for the sisters to send for Jesus. The messengers who bore the report told Jesus, "Lord, the one you love is sick."

Happy is the Christian who has learned to turn to Jesus first in time of sorrow. Unfortunately, Christians often turn to other things and miss the comfort that is rightfully theirs as God's children. Some turn in upon themselves. Something happens in their lives—a death, suffering, disappointment—and they withdraw into a private shell of mourning and contemplation. As a result, there is no victory. Some turn to other people.

There is a degree to which people can help others in times of trouble; their comfort is valuable. God has made men and women mutually dependent; we do need to lean on others and learn from others. That is one reason believers are placed together in a church and are given work by God to do jointly. But there is a limit to what other people can do for us, particularly in time of sorrow, and there is a sense in which people will always disappoint us. The Christian who is spiritually mature, who has lived long with the Lord and known Him and known what He desires of His children, will turn to Jesus and will find in Him one who is truly a friend to the friendless and a father to the fatherless. He is the one who said, "Come to me, all you who are weary and burdened, and I will give you rest" (Matthew 11:28).

THE LORD'S DELAY

Mary and Martha did that. They sent for Jesus, and they waited for Him to come. As they waited, Lazarus's condition grew worse. Expectation turned to eagerness, eagerness to anxiety, and anxiety to despair as their brother died. The source of their hope was absent. They did not know that He had received news of the sickness, had reacted calmly, and had foretold that it would not lead to permanent death but would be an occasion by which the power of God would be known. They knew only that He delayed coming.

John says that after Jesus had received the message of Lazarus's sickness the Lord stayed where He was for two days. Many people have misunderstood the Bible at this point. It has been said on the basis of this text that Jesus delayed His return from the Jordan valley to Bethany in order to let Lazarus die, believing that the resurrection of a dead man would be a greater sign than the healing of a man who was only sick. But that is not the way it actually happened. When Jesus returned to Bethany after the delay of two days He was told that Lazarus had been dead four days. That could only have been possible if Lazarus had died by the time the message of his sickness first reached Jesus. It means that Jesus knew of his death from the beginning and delayed His return for an entirely different purpose.

If that is the case, we must ask again: Why then did Jesus delay a quick return to Bethany? The only answer is that Jesus delayed His return that there might be no doubt Lazarus really was dead and that there might be no cause for doubting the miracle. Jesus also permitted the sorrow of Mary and Martha in order to permit a greater revelation of God's glory. He knew that in His own time He would end it and bring rejoicing.

That leads to the second application of the story. No Christian who has lived with the Lord for any time will say that life, even for a Christian, does not have sorrows. Christians lose loved ones. They endure sickness. They suffer rebuffs and persecutions. They are disappointed in the love of friends and family. But the important thing for the Christian is not that he does not have sorrows but that God knows about them, transforms them, and never permits them to come without a purpose. God is not capricious. He is not weak or inefficient. God always acts in wisdom. Therefore, if some of those things have happened to you, you may know that God has a purpose in them and that He will end them one day in a way that will honor him.

CONTRASTS IN FAITH

The story continues with Jesus' return to Bethany. He did not go directly into the city, since the rulers of the Jews had determined to kill Him and He did not wish His presence known. Instead He waited outside. As He waited, Martha heard that He had come so went to meet Him. Mary waited at home.

In Martha and Mary we have a contrast between two types of faith. When Martha came to Jesus her words contained belief and doubt. She said, "Lord, . . . if you had been here, my brother would not have died. But I know that even now God will give you whatever you ask" (John 11:21-22). Later she said of her brother, "I know he will rise again in the resurrection at the last day" (v. 24). Martha said she knew that God would grant anything Jesus asked of Him. Yet she limited Him to the place and the time. She said, "If you had been *here,* my brother would not have died." She added, "I know he will rise again . . . *at the last day.*"

Martha was a predominantly intellectual believer, as many people are in our day. She had strong character. Her mind was critical. She believed what was reasonable, and she did not profess more than she actually felt. Much of that is good. Christian faith is reasonable; it invites our intellectual assent. Yet there is weakness in mere intellectual assent, for if the whole of our faith is sight, our faith is limited by sight and there is no strength for crises that transcend our understanding. Such faith is always mixed partially with doubt.

Then there is Mary. Her faith was not without reason. She had learned from Jesus. But her faith contained something more. Mary came to Jesus saying the same thing Martha had said: "Lord, if you had been here, my brother would not have died" (John 11:32). But practically every reader recognizes in an instant that it is a quite different cry. Martha had debated with Jesus. Mary fell at His feet, and her words were uttered in the context of total trust and confidence. It was the position Mary loved best. She had sat at His feet when Martha served. She is found at His feet again in John 13.

Mary was the one person who understood that Jesus was going to the cross to die. In chapter 13 she anoints His feet with spikenard, and Jesus testifies that she did that against the day of His burial. Mary had listened. She had learned. But she had gone beyond mere intellectual knowledge to know Jesus intimately and to love him. Out of that love and understanding came the intuitive realization that for Him anything was possible.

THE RESURRECTION

Against this background Jesus taught these women that He was the resurrection and the life. His statement is in John 11:25. It contains two thoughts. First, in Jesus the resurrection is present, for Jesus is Himself life. Martha was thinking in terms of a resurrection at the end of time, a bodily resurrection. Jesus taught that the real resurrection, the one that makes the difference between real life and real death, is the resurrection that takes place when an individual comes face to face with Him. Jesus *is* the resurrection.

If you are a believer in Jesus Christ, you have experienced this resurrection in your life. You were dead in trespasses and sins, and God brought forth life in you by His power as you came in contact with Christ. That is what Jesus meant when He said, "He who believes in me will live, even though he dies; and whoever lives and believes in me will never die." Belief in Him brings spiritual resurrection, what He elsewhere calls the new birth or entrance into everlasting life.

The second great teaching in these verses is that the resurrection at the end of time is a reality as well and is also related to one's relationship to Jesus Christ. Jesus said, "Whoever lives and believes in me *will never die.*" Do you believe that? Do you have the assurance that this promise brings? If so, you may take courage from the fact that Jesus came, not only to save your spirit and soul and guide you in this life, but also to give you a new body that you might live with Him forever, redeemed in body, soul, and spirit, participating in the fullness of the final resurrection.

The story moves to a dramatic conclusion. It is a foretaste, an illustration, of what Christ was promising. Jesus came to the tomb. The people were standing around to see what would happen. The stone was rolled away. Jesus spoke with authority: "Lazarus, come out!" (v. 43), and Lazarus came out bound with grave clothes. The second command was to the people who stood by: "Take off the grave clothes and let him go" (v. 44). The grave clothes were removed, and Lazarus was again with his family.

Do you see the force of this great illustration? It is proof of Christ's power over death, certainly. But it is something more: It is a picture of what God has done for us in Jesus Christ. Apart from Him we are dead in our sins. We are dead men living among dead men. But Christ's voice calls us, bringing life out of death. We hear Him. We emerge from the tomb of a spiritually dead life. Our grave clothes are loosened. We are sent forth to engage in profitable work for Him.

THE FIRST LORD'S DAY

3. Until the Third Day

Enemies of the gospel often understand it better than Christians. They do not believe it, of course. But they do understand it, whereas many Christians, who do believe it, are confused about it.

We have an example in the concern the enemies of Christ took to have the tomb of the newly crucified Christ sealed and guarded by soldiers until the third day. We might think that having accomplished Christ's crucifixion, the leaders of the people would have been satisfied with their work and have returned to business as usual. That is what the disciples were doing as they scattered back to their homes.

But these shrewd enemies of the Lord were different. They remembered Christ's teaching, particularly that part in which He had promised to conquer death and rise again. So they took the steps they thought appropriate.

> The next day, the one after Preparation Day, the chief priests and the Pharisees went to Pilate. "Sir," they said, "we remember that while he was still alive that deceiver said, 'After three days I will rise again.' So give the order for the tomb to be made secure until the third day. Otherwise, his disciples may come and steal the body and tell the people that he has been raised from the dead. This last deception will be worse than the first." (Matthew 27:62-64)

Pilate was probably amused at the request to guard a dead man, but he granted it. "'Take a guard,' Pilate answered. 'Go, make the tomb as secure as you know how.' So they went and made the tomb secure by putting a seal on the stone and posting the guard" (vv. 65-66).

"The third day" takes us back to the trial of Jesus before the Jewish Sanhedrin, where that short phrase was a key element.

There were many illegalities in Christ's trial—the arrest by night, the private interrogation, the absence of a fixed charge before the trial began, the conduct of the trial itself including the intervention of the high priest and the absence of a defense. But the interesting thing is that underneath those illegalities ran a strong undercurrent of legality in the sense of formal adherence to certain points of law.

One of those was the calling of witnesses. Mark says, "Many testified falsely against him, but their statements did not agree" (Mark 14:56). Matthew declares, "The chief priests and the whole Sanhedrin were looking for false evidence against Jesus so that they could put him to death. But they did not find any, though many false witnesses came forward" (Matthew 26:59-60). Apparently, in the opening stages of the trial there was a search for testimony that might have condemned Jesus.

Then something happened. We are told that at last two men offered a piece of evidence that at once put the trial on a new footing. Matthew says that two came forward saying, "This fellow said, 'I am able to destroy the temple of God and rebuild it in three days'" (Matthew 26:61). Mark says that others gave this testimony: "We heard him say, 'I will destroy this man-made temple and in three days will build another, not made by man'" (Mark 14:58). This accusation was obviously of great importance.

First, it was apparently true. At least there was an element of truth in it. The very fact that there were two witnesses who testified to substantially the same thing was one indication of its truthfulness. Again, the fact that the words "in three days" or "on the third day" are repeated often in the gospels is another indication. Jesus apparently made this claim more than once. In fact, of all the details concerning his public teaching and trial, this is perhaps the most frequently repeated idea. The words "the third day" are found twelve times in Matthew, Mark, and Luke, and twice more in the rest of the New Testament. The words "three days" are found ten times in the gospels.

In addition, in one of those unintentional, and therefore particularly striking, corroborations of one or more gospels by another, John actually gives the incident in which these words were first spoken. He says that on the occasion of the first cleansing of the Temple, Jesus, when asked for a sign, replied, "Destroy this temple, and I will raise it again in three days," to which John then remarks, "But the temple he had spoken of was his body" (John 2:19, 21). We notice that although John does not refer to that incident in his own account of the trial, as we might expect him to do, he nevertheless gives us a piece of narration that fits the situation in the other gospels perfectly. Christ's words were spoken publicly in the courtyard of the Temple in Jerusalem and thus before the very types of people who were likely even at that late date to be hanging around the Temple in the service of the scribes and priests.

These three versions of what Jesus said vary in small details. It may be one reason why the testimony was later declared to be invalid. But in spite of the small variations there was obviously something of substance to the testimony.

The second reason this particular indictment was important in the eyes of the priests is that it was also a very serious charge. It was the kind of accusation that, if substantiated, would result in the death penalty. It could have been construed as sorcery, for no one could tear down the Temple and then rebuild it in three days without what we might call "black magic." Or it could be construed as sacrilege; the Temple was the holiest place in Israel. The penalty for both sorcery and sacrilege was death.

As I reflect on this charge, however, I cannot help but feel that Frank Morison is right when he suggests that there was probably more to the issue than even that. For one thing, in spite of the various wordings in which this alleged saying of Jesus is reported, the highly unlikely phrase "in three days" occurs in all versions. Moreover, on some of the other occasions on which this phrase was used, it was perfectly clear that Jesus was prophesying a resurrection of His body three days after he would be put to death. Are we to think that these statements were unknown to the high priests? Are we to think that a man as shrewd as Caiaphas was not aware of what Jesus' enigmatic saying implied? I cannot doubt that they understood precisely what Jesus was claiming, even though they may not have had evidence in a form sufficiently clear to condemn Him legally. They knew that Jesus had said in effect, "You will kill me, but I will prove my divine nature and authority by rising from the dead on the third day."

Morison writes after his own careful development of this position, "I see no escape from the logic of that conclusion. We may hold that he was mistaken; that he was held by some strange mental obsession which periodically flashed out in his public utterance. But that he said this singular and almost unbelievable thing seems to me to be very nearly beyond the possibility of doubt."[1]

That the high priests thus understood Jesus should be demonstrated alone by their later concern to have the tomb guarded.

Fear of Jesus

The concern of the Jewish leaders to have the tomb of Jesus guarded indicates a second item: not only did they understand what Jesus had been saying, they feared Him as well. They might not have said that they feared an actual resurrection (dead men do not rise, do they?), but they certainly feared that something unusual and damaging might happen. What they actually said was, "Give the order for the tomb to be made secure until the third day. Otherwise, his disciples may come and steal the body and tell the people that he has been raised from the dead" (Matthew 27:64).

Was it the disciples, that insignificant band of weak men who did not even stand by their master during His arrest, trial, and crucifixion, whom they feared? Or was it Jesus Himself who terrified them?

I believe that the leaders' use of Judas in Jesus' arrest shows that they actually

1. Frank Morison, *Who Moved the Stone?* (Downers Grove, Ill.: InterVarsity, 1969), p. 24. First edition 1930.

feared the Master. For why was Judas necessary if they did not fear Him? Usually, two explanations of Judas's role are given: either that Judas was necessary in order to lead the arresting party to Christ's hiding place during those last days, or else that he was necessary to assure a secret arrest because of the leaders' fear of the people. But that is not as clear a matter as one might suppose. Frank Morison has pointed out, "To regard Judas merely as a common informer, ready (for a consideration) to lead the authorities to the secret hiding-place of his erstwhile friend and leader, is absurd."[2] For Jesus was not in hiding. In fact, He could hardly have been more open. There had been a time in which He had removed Himself from the vicinity of Jerusalem, knowing that His hour was not yet fully come (John 11:54). But from the moment He had arrived in Bethany from Jericho on the Friday preceding His crucifixion no attempt seems to have been made to conceal His movements. The raising of Lazarus, which took place on that day, was done openly. On the next day, Saturday, many came to see Him and talk both to Him and to Lazarus. On Sunday, Jesus entered Jerusalem with great display while those who were with Him and those who came out from the city to greet Him cried out, "Hosanna! Blessed is he who comes in the name of the Lord! Blessed is the King of Israel!" (John 12:13). On Monday, Tuesday, and Wednesday He had traveled back and forth openly.

Under these circumstances, how could it be that the leaders of the people needed Judas, and were even willing to pay him money, to tell them where Jesus was? If they had felt free to arrest Jesus, the leaders could have done so in Jerusalem at nearly any unguarded moment. Or they could easily have sent to Bethany and effected His arrest there.

It is common at this point to introduce the other explanation of Judas's role: to allow them to arrest Christ in secret for fear of the people. But that is at best a half-truth. There was undoubtedly a real fear on the part of the chief priests and Pharisees of what the people might do. There was fear of a disturbance that might cause the intervention of the Roman armies with dire consequences for them. Even greater was their fear that the multitudes in Jerusalem might actually believe on Jesus. Earlier the leaders had said, "What are we accomplishing? . . . Here is this man performing many miraculous signs. If we let him go on like this, everyone will believe in him, and then the Romans will come and take away both our place and our nation" (John 11:47-48). Out of that council had come the decision to have Jesus killed. But certainly there were other times when these leaders might have taken Jesus secretly—in Bethany in the early morning or late evening, on the road between Bethany and Jerusalem, in a quiet corner of the capital, even in the upper room. That they did not do that, but rather relied on Judas to bring them information necessary to achieve the arrest, suggests that there were other factors involved.

2. *Ibid.*, p. 30.

Is it not the case—is this not the best explanation of these confusing elements—that they actually feared *Jesus?* They had tried to arrest Him on other occasions. Once a body of officers, who were probably Temple guards, was dispatched by the chief priests to take Him. They returned with the task undone. "Why didn't you bring him in?" they were asked.

Their reply was incredible: "No one ever spoke the way this man does" (John 7:46).

Later another attempt was made, this time to stone Him. "But Jesus," we are told, "hid himself, slipping away from the temple grounds" (John 8:59). A third time we are told that "they tried to seize him, but he escaped their grasp" (John 10:39).

What would these men have been thinking as a result of their abortive attempts to take Jesus? Probably they would not have voiced their most fundamental fear, even to themselves. But they must have been fearing—because of Christ's obvious power and their own earlier failures—that in the ultimate analysis He might perhaps be unarrestable? *Unarrestable!* If that were the case, it would explain their failure to do anything during the earlier part of that last Passover week, their final abrupt decision which very nearly failed, and their use of Judas (not to tell them where Jesus was, but to bring them reports of His moods and alert them to when He just might be willing to submit to an arrest). Judas would have said, "I think the mood of surrender is upon Him. He has been talking about death. If you move quickly, I think He might go with you. Hurry, I will take you to Him." On the basis of that information the leaders launched the sudden events of Christ's trial.

These actions show us the religious leaders' fear of Jesus. So we are not surprised to see that what had governed their actions earlier was still gripping them. They had been worried, and they were still worried. They were afraid that even after He was dead something might happen to vindicate Him and secure their loss and condemnation.

DAY OF RESURRECTION

But that was what happened anyway! They got their guard. They sealed the tomb, but Jesus could not be so bound. Thus, with the completion of His prophesied three days' sleep in death, He broke the seal, scattered the guard, and rose triumphant.

> Vainly they watch his bed—Jesus, my Saviour;
> Vainly they seal the dead—Jesus, my Lord.
>
> Up from the grave he arose,
> With a mighty triumph o'er his foes.
> He arose a victor from the dark domain,
> And he lives forever with his saints to reign.
> He arose! He arose! Hallelujah! Christ arose!

Moreover, Jesus made that day—the day the Jewish leaders feared and guarded against—not just another day, but rather the new day of Christian worship, activity, and joyous celebration.

Have you ever noticed that beginning with the resurrection every event recorded in the New Testament that had important religious significance fell on the first day of the week, the Lord's Day? This has been pointed out by Lewis Sperry Chafer in his book entitled *Grace*.[3]

There are eleven events:

1. The first and obviously the most important is that on the first day of the week *Jesus arose from the dead*. This fact is mentioned in all the gospels and is referred to constantly throughout the rest of the New Testament.

2. On the first day of the week the *Lord Jesus ascended into heaven for the first time*. We find the record in John 20:17, in which Jesus said to Mary Magdalene, "Do not hold on to me, for I have not yet returned to the Father. Go instead to my brothers and tell them, 'I am returning to my Father and your Father, to my God and your God.'" Jesus did not spend the forty days between the events of Easter morning and His final ascension to heaven darting around the countryside trying to hide behind rocks or trees and then appearing suddenly for a few moments in what are the recorded appearances of the Lord to His disciples. During those days Jesus passed freely between earth and heaven.

3. On the first day of the week *Jesus appeared to the disciples for the first time while they were in the upper room and there bestowed peace upon them*. Peace is one of the three great results of justification listed by the apostle Paul in the fifth chapter of Romans. He speaks of peace, access to God, and rejoicing. Christ gave these gifts to the disciples. They had not been at peace. They were not aware of God's presence. They were certainly not rejoicing, for we are told that they were gathered together in secret for fear of the Jews. Jesus changed the state of mind of each of them by His presence.

4. On the first day of the week *Jesus first broke bread with His disciples*. This happened twice, once in the presence of the two disciples whom He had overtaken on the road to Emmaus, and once in the upper room with all the disciples at the end of the first Lord's Day. These were the first post-resurrection observances of the Communion service.

5. On the first day of the week *Jesus opened the understanding of the disciples* so that they might know all that the Scriptures had taught concerning Him (Luke 24:45-47).

6. On the first day of the week *Jesus commissioned the disciples to the task of world evangelism*. He said in John 20:21, "As the Father has sent me, I am sending you." We read in Luke 24:48 that He said, "You are witnesses of these things."

3. Lewis Sperry Chafer, *Grace* (Chicago: The Bible Institute Colportage Association, 1939), pp. 272-76.

7. On the first day of the week *Jesus breathed on the disciples, imparting the Holy Spirit to them* (John 20:22).

8. On the first day of the week, seven weeks after the resurrection, at Pentecost, *the Holy Spirit descended from heaven* and began His ministry for the entire age of the Christian church.

9. On the first day of the week *the Holy Spirit directed Paul to gather the believers together and preach to them.* The story is told in Acts 20. It concerns a period of Paul's life when he was pursuing missionary work at Troas.

10. The first day of the week was established by Paul as the day on which *each believer was to "set aside a sum of money in keeping with his income"* (1 Corinthians 16:2). It was the day on which offerings were to be taken and dedicated to the Lord's work.

11. Finally, on the first day of the week *the Lord Jesus Christ appeared to the apostle John on the island of Patmos* and gave a revelation of Himself in His present heavenly glory. The same revelation also outlined His plans for the future, for the church age, and for the period that will follow His coming again.

The listing of these eleven events shows the importance of the day of the resurrection for the church. It is important as the day of our Lord's resurrection and has set the pattern for our present Christian celebration. Everything we do on Sunday is based on these events: the gathering of ourselves together, the reading and interpretation of the Scriptures, preaching and teaching, the collecting of offerings, the observance of communion, and above all the remembrance and worship of the One who died for us and rose again. We do not do these things by accident or by whim—it is God's pattern. We follow it out of thanksgiving for what God has done for us through the victory of our Lord.

4. As Safe As You Know How

Usually the Bible is not an amusing book. The issues with which it deals are too grave. But the Bible is an honest book, and when it reports situations in life that are naturally funny it reflects them honestly and therefore with an appropriate sense of humor.

There is a situation like that in Matthew's account of the death and burial of Jesus Christ, preceding his resurrection. For months the chief priests and Pharisees, who were the rulers of Israel, had been stalking Jesus, and they had at last attained His execution at the hands of Pilate, the Roman governor. Jesus had died on the day before the Passover and had been quickly buried. In any other situation that should have been the story's end. But the leaders remembered that Jesus has foretold his resurrection, and therefore they came to Pilate with the request that he make Jesus' tomb secure. "Otherwise," they said, "his disciples may come and steal the body and tell the people that he has been raised from the dead. This last deception will be worse than the first."

Pilate replied—I am sure it must have been in jest—"Take a guard. Go, make the tomb as secure as you know how." So they secured the tomb by putting a seal on it and posting a guard (Matthew 27:62-66).

What did Pilate have in mind when he told the leaders, "Go, make the tomb as secure as you know how"? It must have been one of two things, as Matthew Henry, one of the great old biblical expositors, suggests. Either Pilate was laughing at the priests for their folly—imagine setting a guard to watch a dead man!—or, more likely, he was mocking them for their fears. It was as though he were saying, "Do your worst, try your wit and strength to the utmost; but if He be of God, He will rise in spite of you and all your guards."[1]

---

1. Matthew Henry, *Matthew Henry's Commentary on the Whole Bible*, vol. 5, *Matthew to John* (New York, London and Edinburgh: Revell Company, n.d.), p. 436.

That is what Charles Haddon Spurgeon, well-known Baptist preacher of the nineteenth century, thought the text meant. He almost laughed himself as he described the chief priests begging "*Pilate* to do what he could to prevent the rising of their victim."[2]

A Violent Earthquake

When the chief priests and Pharisees came to the Roman governor they explained their request by saying: "Otherwise, his disciples may come and steal the body and tell the people that he has been raised from the dead" (v. 64). But that is not what they truly feared, as we saw in the last chapter. For one thing, the disciples were not worth fearing. Doubt on that score had been settled at the time of Christ's arrest in the garden when those "stouthearted companions" forsook their Master and fled back over the Mount of Olives to Bethany. Apparently, only Peter and John made it to Jerusalem to witness the crucifixion, and neither of them was of any help to Jesus. Peter even denied his Lord. If the priests had really feared the disciples, it would have been an easy matter to have arrested them at the same time they arrested Jesus or at least to have rounded them up shortly afterward. That they did not do so indicates that they (rightly) had no fears on their account.

What did they fear then? In my judgment, what they actually feared was the resurrection. They were not imperceptive. They had been observing Jesus for the better part of three years. They had seen Him heal the sick, give sight to the blind, cleanse the lepers, restore strength to the impotent. Then, greatest wonder of all, only a few days before His arrest He had actually raised Lazarus of Bethany from the grave.

There was no use denying the miracles. They tried to deny them at first, but there were too many miracles and too many witnesses to do that convincingly. Toward the end they simply acknowledged the miracles but attributed them to the devil. This man—this miracle worker—claimed that three days after He had been crucified He would be raised from death by God. Were they not afraid that He who had raised Lazarus would Himself conquer death and shatter their little ecclesiastical world forever?

So they did their best. First, they sealed the stone that had been rolled over the mouth of the tomb. Oh, what authority was there! Who would dare to break that seal, thus setting himself against the united political and spiritual powers of their state? Second, they posted guards, guards from the same company that had arrested Jesus in the garden. These were their officers, Jews. Surely they could be trusted.

The guard was set. The hours and days rolled by. All seemed well.

Suddenly "there was a violent earthquake, for an angel of the Lord came down

2. Charles Haddon Spurgeon, *The Gospel of the Kingdom: A Popular Exposition of the Gospel According to Matthew* (Pasadena, Tex.: Pilgrim Publications, 1974), p. 253.

from heaven and, going to the tomb, rolled back the stone and sat on it. His appearance was like lightning, and his clothes were white as snow. The guards were so afraid of him that they shook and became like dead men" (Matthew 28:2-4). The seal was broken! The tomb was empty! Christ was not there! He was risen! The guards were scattered. The rule of the Pharisees and priests was broken, and Christianity began its triumphant expansion into God's world!

"Go, make the tomb as secure as you know how." Secure against God? Secure against the life-shattering power of the resurrection?

A BLINDING LIGHT

A few years after Christ's resurrection a distinguished young rabbi rose to prominence. He had studied under Gamaliel and had achieved stature among the Pharisees, the very sect that had been instrumental in securing the death of the hated Nazarene. Christianity had not died out after Jesus' crucifixion, and this young rabbi—his name was Saul of Tarsus—determined to stamp it out forceably. He rooted out the Christians of Jerusalem, and when he found them he saw that they were arrested and executed. Not satisfied with his work in Jerusalem, he went to the high priest to secure letters of introduction to the synagogues in Damascus so that if he found any there who were Christians he might arrest them and bring them to Jerusalem for trial.

Saul was in the company of those who had tried to secure the tomb of Jesus years before, and he was trying to secure two things. First, he was trying to secure Judaism from the explosive vitality of the Nazarene's new sect. He regarded Christianity as a heresy and Jesus as a blasphemer and child of Satan. By arresting Christians he hoped to secure his own religion.

Second, he was trying desperately to secure himself. Later, he realized that he was trying to "kick against the goads" (Acts 26:14) like an animal fighting one who is prodding it to go in a right direction. This meant that, although Saul was fighting against the Christians with intense zeal, he was at the same time fighting an even more intense struggle within the secret chambers of his heart. In fact, his outward zeal may be explained by his internal struggle. Saul had given his life to Judaism. But suppose the Christians were right? Suppose Jesus really was the incarnate Son of God? Suppose He really was the Messiah and that His death on the cross was God's own vicarious sacrifice for His people's sins? Suppose Jesus really had risen from the dead? Saul must not think about that. Not that! On with the work! Forward against the Christians!

In this divided state of mind Saul was making his way northward from Jerusalem to Damascus when suddenly a bright light flashed about him and he fell blinded to the ground. Those who were traveling with Saul saw the light and heard a voice, but only Saul understood what was said.

"Saul, Saul, why do you persecute me?"

"Who are you, Lord?" Saul asked. The way in which he answered the speaker showed that Saul sensed what was coming.

"I am Jesus, whom you are persecuting," the voice replied. "Now get up and go into the city, and you will be told what you must do" (Acts 9:1-6). When Saul, now Paul, obeyed and went into Damascus, God sent a disciple named Ananias to confirm him in faith and tell him of God's call to world evangelism: "This man is my chosen instrument to carry my name before the Gentiles and their kings and before the people of Israel. I will show him how much he must suffer for my name" (Acts 9:15-16). This persecutor of Christians became the first great Christian missionary.

Saul's heart had said, "Go, make your ancient religion, its traditions, your heart, as secure as you know how." In the midst of letters, arrests, trials, and executions it said, "Make yourself secure against Jesus. Stamp Him out with your activity. Subdue Him by your zeal."

But suddenly—there was a bright light, and the resurrection became reality.

A Thriving Fellowship

Someone else was interested in securing his interests against the resurrection, although he had actually been leading the battle against Jesus Christ all along. His name is Satan. We first saw him in the Garden of Eden, where he tempted Eve to eat the forbidden fruit. We saw him in Egypt, where anti-Semitism originated. We saw him in countless persecutions against those through whom the Messiah was to come. At last we see him waging war against the incarnate Jesus.

At the time of Christ's birth it was Satan who stirred up the evil imaginations of Herod to murder the babes of Bethlehem, thinking by that means to secure himself against Christ. At the time of Christ's baptism Satan appeared openly to tempt the Lord to sin.

> If you are the Son of God, tell these stones to become bread. . . . If you are the Son of God . . . throw yourself down. For it is written:
>
> > "He will command his angels concerning you,
> > and they will lift you up in their hands,
> > so that you will not strike your foot against a stone."
>
> . . . All this I will give you . . . if you will bow down and worship me. (Matthew 4:3, 6, 9)

Later in Christ's ministry Satan moved the rulers of the Jews against Him. He even got Judas to betray Christ and the other disciples to forsake him.

What a triumph Satan must have imagined as he goaded the people to cry out: "Crucify him! Crucify him!" What glee he must have felt as the governor's judgment was pronounced and the one he hated most in all the universe was led to crucifixion. What delight he must have nurtured as the rough nails were forced through Jesus' feet and hands and the friend of sinners eventually weakened and died. What bliss when Christ was buried. What ecstasy when the Master's gray, lifeless body was sealed in Joseph's tomb. Satan had won! The devil had killed God's Son. He had secured his evil kingdom against the second Person of the divine Trinity.

Yes, yes! Satan had made his plans as secure as he knew how! But when the resurrection came he was no more effective than the soliders in their attempt to resist the Lord of glory.

But Satan did not give up there. Indeed, to this day he has not given up. Though defeated, Satan still works against the power of the resurrected one. He persecutes the church. When Jewish persecution (such as that of Saul of Tarsus) was insufficient, he engaged the strength of Rome and after that the powers of the state in most lands.

John Foxe's *Book of Martyrs* is the most important book ever written on the persecution of the church of Jesus Christ.[3] Foxe wrote during the days of Queen Elizabeth to document the persecutions of English believers during the reigns of the preceding English monarchs. But he began at the beginning, noting on the first page that when Peter made his confession that Jesus was the "Son of the living God" Jesus replied, "On this rock I will build my church, and the gates of Hades will not overcome it" (Matthew 16:18). Foxe took this to teach: 1) that Christ will have a church in this world, 2) that not only the world but also the utmost strength and powers of hell should be arrayed against it, and 3) that notwithstanding the utmost hatred and malice of the devil the church would remain and prosper until Christ's return for it.

That has happened. Whipped to fury by the resurrection and subsequent outpouring of the Holy Spirit, Satan stirred the world to despise and persecute Christians. The first of the great persecutions was during the reign of Nero, when thousands were burned as human torches or fed to wild animals in the arena. Under Decius and Valerian the opposition spread throughout the Empire. In those days (A.D. 249 and 258) it became a crime to convert to Christianity, and those who were already Christians had their lands confiscated.

In A.D. 303 Diocletian began the fiercest and longest of the persecutions. He too made it a crime to be a Christian. He circulated false documents purporting to explain the faith of the believers as a fraud. He reactivated the old pagan cults, reorganizing them along "Christian" lines. Diocletian encouraged popular movements against the church and caused the death of many. In the reign of Julian "the Apostate" (A.D. 361 to 363) the same tactics were repeated.

Hatred. Persecutions. Banishment. Murders. Those were the weapons by

---

3. My edition is in eight volumes, containing Foxe's original twelve books plus background material on Foxe himself: *The Acts and Monuments of John Foxe*, ed. Stephen Reed Cattley (London: R. B. Seeley and W. Burnside, 1841).

which the prince of darkness attempted to make his realm secure against the expanding forces of God's anointed King.

"Make it as secure as you can"? Satan was trying, but it was no use. Jesus had risen, and the thriving fellowship of His followers was advancing through the world.

AN INESCAPABLE SURRENDER

I wonder if you have been confronted by the power of the resurrection. The chief priests and Pharisees tried to secure their ecclesiastical world against Jesus. Saul tried to secure his religious traditions. Satan has been trying to secure his own evil kingdom. Perhaps you have been trying to secure your own way of doing things or your own values or your own mastery of your time. You have heard Christ's gospel, but you have tried to keep Him politely in His place.

Jesus is not that easily contained. You push Him back, but He comes forward again. You banish Him but He intrudes when you are least expecting it. What are you going to do against the resurrection power of the one so many call Lord? How are you going to make yourself secure against Jesus?

Let me suggest what you can do. You can begin with activity. That should not be too difficult in our country and in our time. Our world seems preoccupied with activity and even rewards those who are busiest. If you are busy enough, you will not have time to think. Fill your time. Schedule your idle hours. Take a class in art or foreign languages or computers or aerobics or any one of a thousand other things. Then you will not have to go to Bible study. You can claim that you are too busy when a Christian friend invites you. Play golf or racket ball on Sundays, or join a group that jogs during the Sunday morning hours. Then you will not have to go to church. Above all, fill your evenings with television programs or the latest best seller. Then you will not have to read the Bible.

Second, you can fill your life with pleasure, particularly if it is of a sinful kind. Jesus is the sinless Son of God, and sin will keep you from Him. Fill your life with sin's pleasures. Make it as secure as you can against Jesus.

I have one more suggestion. You can become religious. Religion is a great defense against true godliness. But if you take this course, I suggest that you do not learn too much about Christianity. Instead, submerge yourself in ceremony. Do things, not because they are meaningful—you might have to think about the meaning—but for tradition's sake or for mere aesthetics. Yes, that will help. Go, make your life as secure as you can with religion. Attach your seals! Post your guards! Erect your barricades!

Alas, I am afraid it will not be enough. Jesus has broken seals before. He has scattered countless guards. What will you do when the light bursts forth from heaven and the voice asks you, "Saul, John, Mary, Albert, Susan, why do you persecute me?" What will you do when the tomb springs open and Jesus of Nazareth confronts you in resurrected splendor?

I will tell you what I would do. I would give up fighting. I would lay down my seals and stones and guards and feverish activity. I would lay aside my sins. I would fall down before Him and say, as Thomas said, "My Lord and my God." Then He will make you His, and He will tell you what you are to do and be for His sake.

5. Rewards Instead of Punishments

*I*t is an interesting feature of the resurrection of Jesus Christ that the event was known to the enemies of the Lord before it was known to His friends. The resurrection took place before dawn on what we call Easter Sunday. When the women arrived at the tomb at dawn the stone had been removed, and the tomb was already empty (Luke 24:1-2; John 20:1). Since the soldiers had been at the tomb when the angel descended and rolled the stone away, they, rather than the women, were the first to know of this occurrence. Matthew tells us that while the women were on their way to tell Peter and John that they had seen angels who had announced that Christ was risen, the soldiers were reporting the same thing to the elders and chief priests.

I wonder if the enemies of the Lord had been sleeping peacefully that Saturday night. They might have been, because they thought that they had got rid of the one who had threatened to turn their world upside down and demolish their traditions. Yet they had feared the resurrection. If they had been sleeping fitfully, I suppose their worst nightmares were suddenly confirmed by the insistent early knocking of the soldiers and by their reports of the empty tomb.

The people who really interest me in this story are the soldiers. They had been frightened by the angel so that, as the story says, "they shook and became like dead men" (Matthew 28:4). But their fear could hardly have been much less after the angel had departed and they had left the tomb—which it was now pointless to guard—to report to the authorities. They had failed in their assignment. That was a serious failure for soldiers in that time. In some cases such failures were punishable by death. Besides, the priests had impressed on them how important it was to guard the tomb, lest something happen that might give the disciples cause to proclaim a resurrection. These were powerful men, men to be feared. Were the soldiers not to expect the most dreadful of punishments? Were they not to be beaten or even killed for their failures?

I can picture these men trembling in the anteroom of the priests' quarters, wondering what was to happen to them. Suddenly the door opened. But instead of harsh words, they were met with a conspiratorial tone. They were to be part of a cover-up, and they were to be rewarded for their part. The text says,

> When the chief priests had met with the elders and devised a plan, they gave the soldiers a large sum of money, telling them, "You are to say, 'His disciples came during the night and stole him away while we were asleep.' If this report gets to the governor, we will satisfy him and keep you out of trouble." So the soldiers took the money and did as they were instructed. (Matthew 28:12-15)

That was the first attempt to explain away the resurrection.

A FOOLISH STORY

The explanation was foolish of course. Even the soldiers, who no doubt were not terribly well-educated men, would have known it was ludicrous. For one thing, they were to say the disciples had stolen the body of Jesus *while they were sleeping.* But if they were sleeping, how would they have known that it was the disciples who had stolen the body? Perhaps one soldier at least had been awake and had seen the disciples. But then, why had he not immediately awakened the others and driven the disciples off? The idea of a ragtag bag of Galilean peasants, as most of the disciples were, being able to outwit or overpower a band of armed soldiers was ridiculous. Perhaps the soldiers only suspected the disciples. In that case, why did they not get onto their tracks at once? It should not have been too hard to track the disciples down, expose the theft, and recover the body.

John Calvin wrote, "It was a childish excuse that would not have gotten them off for nothing if they had been dealing with an upright judicious governor."[1] But that is just the point. Neither the governor, the priests, nor the scribes were upright. The sign of the prophet Jonah had just been brought to them in the clearest of all possible ways and from a most unimpeachable source; the soldiers had everything to lose and nothing to gain by their story. Yet these enemies of the Lord were committed in advance to unbelief. They did not disbelieve because of a lack of evidence. They disbelieved and therefore suppressed the evidence.

Thus, lies were devised and promulgated, and the soldiers—who agreed to go along with the plan—received rewards instead of punishments.

REWARDS OF UNBELIEF

It has been the same ever since. I think of the nineteenth century and of a well-known scholar by the name of Ernest Renan (1823-1892). He came from a relatively poor family from the French province of Breton. He was educated in conservative Catholicism and became a priest. But he fell in with liberal

1. John Calvin, *A Harmony of the Gospels Matthew, Mark and Luke,* vol. 3, trans. by A. W. Morrison (Grand Rapids: Eerdmans, 1972), p. 230.

scholarship, as so many brilliant young men have, and before long he was pursuing the thoughts of Georg Friedrich Hegel and Emmanuel Kant with rigor. He was enamoured with rationalism and tried to look at the gospel accounts from that perspective. In time Renan produced a *Life of Jesus* in which he explained away belief in the resurrection. He attributed it to the impassioned hallucination of Mary Magdalene. He argued that Mary was in love with Jesus, was mentally unstable, and therefore imagined she had seen Him and had heard Him call her name, when actually she had only seen the gardener.

Renan's views were a radical denial of Christian doctrine. He should have been censored for his unbelief. But he was not! Instead, he became the darling of the Parisian salons, was made an administrator of the prestigious Collège de France, and was appointed a grand officer of the Legion of Honor. His *Life of Jesus* sold sixty thousand copies in its first months.

For a contemporary example we have the story of Hugh J. Schonfield, a Jewish historian from Britain, who in 1966 published a bizarre interpretation of the life and death of Jesus called *The Passover Plot*. It maintained that Jesus was aware of Old Testament prophecies about a dying and rising Messiah and therefore manipulated people and events to fulfill them. He planned to be crucified, according to Schonfield. But he had confided in Joseph of Arimathea, Lazarus, a Judean priest, and an anonymous "young man," with whose help he plotted to feign a resurrection. The conspirators were to give Jesus a drug so that he could appear to have died. (It was in the vinegar or cheap wine that was given to Him on the cross.) Then they were to entomb but later recover and revive the body, after which Jesus would present himself as having been resurrected.

But the plot failed. It failed because of the unexpected spear wound that Jesus received from a soldier. Schonfield wrote,

> What seems probable is that in the darkness of Saturday night, when Jesus was brought out of the tomb by those concerned in the plan, he regained consciousness temporarily but finally succumbed. If, as the Fourth Gospel says, his side was pierced by a lance before he was taken from the cross, his chances of recovery were slender. It was much too risky, and perhaps too late, to take the body back to the tomb, replace the bandages left there, roll the stone across the entrance and try to create the impression that everything was as it had been on Friday evening. It would also have been thought most unseemly. Before dawn the mortal remains of Jesus were quickly yet reverently interred, leaving the puzzle of the empty tomb.[2]

Schonfield explained the resurrection "appearances" as cases of mistaken identity.

A theory as strange as this understandably made little impact on the scholarly community, even among men disinclined to accept the resurrection. But, strikingly, it received widespread attention in the media and much extravagant

---

2. Hugh J. Schonfield, *The Passover Plot: New Light on the History of Jesus* (New York: Bantam, 1967), p. 165.

praise by clerics. *The Passover Plot* sold over 100,000 copies in the first five months and went through eleven printings in less than two years.

Harold Blake Walker, a Presbyterian pastor, wrote a complimentary review for the *Chicago Tribune* in which he called the book "Fascinating. . . . Lucidly written and carefully documented. . . . A valuable addition."

Saturday Review wrote, "Sensational. . . . Bound to stir readers. . . . For all the audacity of its central thesis, his book is always scholarly. . . . Buttressed with research."

William Barclay, the well-known author of *The Daily Study Bible*, called it "a book of enormous learning and erudition, meticulously documented. . . . It demands to be read."

Daniel A. Poling, editor of the *Christian Herald,* said, "The author reveals himself as a more careful student of the New Testament than many Christians who read it devotionally."[3]

Here is a case in which a most bizarre explaining away of the resurrection received not a well-deserved rebuff or ridicule, as one might have expected, but praise—and that even from distinguished Christian editors and scholars.

TRUTH PERSECUTED

Think now of the other characters in the resurrection story: the women who first went to the tomb, Peter and John who ran there after hearing the women's reports, the Emmaus disciples, and then the other followers of Jesus. These not only heard the reports; they saw Jesus. In fact, so many saw Jesus alive after the resurrection that the apostle Paul would later write of this company: "He appeared to Peter, and then to the Twelve. After that, he appeared to more than five hundred of the brothers at the same time, most of whom are still living, though some have fallen asleep. Then he appeared to James, then to all the apostles, and last of all he appeared to me also, as to one abnormally born" (1 Corinthians 15:5-8).

These people knew the truth about the resurrection. They proclaimed it widely, and what they proclaimed was good news: Jesus was raised, death was defeated, salvation was assured. But were these people welcomed for their preaching? On the contrary, although they spoke the truth and not lies, they received punishments instead of rewards.

Peter and John were first. After waiting in Jerusalem for the coming of the Holy Spirit, they began to preach the good news: "This man was handed over to you by God's set purpose and foreknowledge; and you, with the help of wicked men, put him to death by nailing him to the cross. But God raised him from the dead, freeing him from the agony of death, because it was impossible for death to keep its

---

3. These review comments are taken from the inside and back covers of the 1967 Bantam edition.

hold on him" (Acts 2:23-24). Word of this preaching reached the religious leaders, and they were greatly disturbed, as well they may have been. They arrested the apostles, put them in prison, and interrogated them. At last they commanded them "not to speak or teach at all in the name of Jesus" and threatened punishment if they should do so (see Acts 4:18-21). However, when they let Peter and John go, the two men immediately returned to their preaching.

They were arrested again. This time God sent an angel to open the doors of the jail. The next morning, when the high priest and his associates arrived to begin their trial of the apostles, they were told that the jail was empty and the men who had been jailed were again in the Temple courts teaching the people (Acts 5:17-25).

The apostles were arrested a third time and, when asked to account for their refusal to heed the priestly ban on preaching, they said: "The God of our fathers raised Jesus from the dead—whom you had killed by hanging him on a tree. God exalted him to his own right hand as Prince and Savior that he might give repentance and forgiveness of sins to Israel. We are witnesses of these things, and so is the Holy Spirit, whom God has given to those who obey him" (Acts 5:30-32). That made the authorities furious. They flogged the apostles, but they "left the Council chamber rejoicing that God had counted them worthy to suffer dishonor for his Name" (v. 41).

Not long after that a harsher punishment fell on another of God's choice servants: Stephen, one of the first deacons. He was arrested for blasphemy and was placed on trial. At his trial Stephen gave a long recital of Israel's resistance to the Holy Spirit's teaching, concluding with the accusation that the leaders had killed God's Son. At that point God gave Stephen a vision in which he saw Jesus standing at the right hand of God. He testified to that, saying, "Look, . . . I see heaven open and the Son of Man standing at the right hand of God" (Acts 7:56). It so infuriated his interrogators that they immediately dragged him out of the city and stoned him to death.

I think too of Paul. Paul was the first great missionary to the Gentiles, and we would suppose perhaps that in Gentile lands—far from the super-heated, volatile atmosphere of Jerusalem—the gospel of a crucified but risen Lord would be more tolerantly received. Yet it was not. When God called Paul he said to Ananias, who helped in the recovery of Paul's sight, "I will show him how much he must suffer for my name" (Acts 9:16). Paul did suffer. He suffered dangers and ridicule, stonings and imprisonment, and eventually death at the hands of the secular authorities. Paul wrote about it on one occasion:

> I have worked much harder, been in prison more frequently, been flogged more severely, and been exposed to death again and again. Five times I received from the Jews the forty lashes minus one. Three times I was beaten with rods, once I was stoned, three times I was shipwrecked, I spend a night and a day in the open sea, I have been constantly on the move. I have been in danger from rivers, in danger from bandits, in

danger from my own countrymen, in danger from Gentiles; in danger in the city, in danger in the country, in danger at sea; and in danger from false brothers. I have labored and toiled and have often gone without sleep; I have known hunger and thirst and have often gone without food; I have been cold and naked. Besides everything else, I face daily the pressure of my concern for all the churches. (2 Corinthians 11:23-28)

Paul preached Jesus, but he received no earthly rewards. Instead, he received what most would call punishments.

THE TABLES TURNED

Why should anybody endure such punishments? Why should Paul have kept preaching when all it brought him was suffering? Was Stephen's martyrdom worth it? What was the point of Peter and John's flogging at the hands of the Sanhedrin? Would it not have been better for each of them if they had simply gone with the tide and done what the Jewish leaders wanted? Would it not have been wiser to do as the soldiers, who took the money and kept silent?

Silent about Jesus? About the resurrection? Each of those early Christians would tell us that they could never have kept silent, because the message they proclaimed was no mere earthly message that could be believed or not, depending upon whether it proved beneficial or instead required sacrifice. The resurrection is not philosophy. It is a fact of history. Therefore, as Peter and John replied to the Sanhedrin, they could not "help speaking about what [they had] seen and heard" (Acts 4:20).

And there is this fact also. In this life the tables are often turned so that truth suffers and lies are praised. But this life is not the full limit of reality, any more than the tomb of Joseph of Arimathea was the end of the line for Jesus Christ. Jesus lives! And so truth lives, regardless of man's opposition to it. In this life the deceiver may receive rewards. It has happened before; it will happen again. But in the life to come truth will be rewarded, evil will be punished and those who have served the risen Christ will hear Him declare, "Well done, good and faithful servant! . . . Come and share your master's happiness!" (Matthew 25:21).

6. The Not-Quite-Empty Tomb

One of the great historical evidences of the resurrection of Jesus Christ is the empty tomb. But the remarkable and quite startling fact is that when Peter and John arrived at the tomb on the first Easter morning it was not quite empty. The body of Jesus was gone, but something was still there. The graveclothes remained behind. The Bible suggests that there was something so striking about them that John saw them and immediately believed in Jesus' resurrection.

That is significant, for it marks the first time there was an indication of belief by one of the disciples. As we saw earlier, Ernest Renan argued that faith in the resurrection was the result of the rumors spread by Mary Magdalene who had suffered a hallucination, thinking she had seen Jesus. But that could not be. Mary suffered no hallucination. The last thing in the world she expected was the resurrection of her Lord. And John, at least, testified that he believed some time before Mary ever returned to the tomb and met Jesus in the garden.

EVENTS OF EASTER MORNING

The time element is of great interest here. It provides valuable background to the experiences of Peter and John at the tomb. Critics have made much of the so-called discrepancies in the gospel accounts, but there are no discrepancies when the accounts are correctly understood.

Jesus had been crucified either on Friday (as the church has generally believed) or else on Thursday (which is less widely held but which seems to fit the evidence). Regardless, Jesus lay in the tomb until the resurrection, which certainly took place before dawn on Sunday morning. At that point the women came to the tomb from Jerusalem bearing spices to anoint the body. There were at least four women and probably more. Matthew says that the group included Mary Magdalene and the other Mary, that is, Mary the mother of James. Mark adds that

Salome was present. Luke says that Joanna was also along and others. The women started out while it was still dark and arrived at the tomb in the early dawn while it was still difficult to distinguish objects.

On reaching the tomb the women were astonished to find the stone removed from the entrance. We must imagine them standing about, afraid to go too close, wondering what had happened. Who moved the stone? Had the tomb been pilfered? Had the body of Jesus been stolen? Had Joseph of Arimathea removed it to another place? What were they to do? At last they decided that the disciples must be told, and Mary Magdalene was dispatched to find them. Not one of them imagined that Jesus had been raised from the dead.

After a while it began to grow a little lighter, and the women grew bolder. They decided to look into the tomb. There they saw angels. The women were afraid. But an angel said, "Do not be afraid, for I know that you are looking for Jesus, who was crucified. He is not here; he has risen, just as he said. Come and see the place where he lay. Then go quickly and tell his disciples" (Matthew 28:5-7).

Mary meanwhile found the two chief disciples, Peter and John, presumably in John's house where the beloved disciple had taken Mary on the day of the crucifixion (John 19:27).

The two disciples immediately started for the tomb, running and leaving Mary far behind. John was the younger man. Consequently he arrived at the tomb first, stooped to look through the narrow opening and saw the graveclothes. Then Peter arrived, out of breath and in a hurry as usual; he brushed John aside and plunged into the tomb. When John saw the graveclothes, he saw them only in a cursory manner and from outside the tomb. The Greek uses the most common word for seeing. But when Peter arrived he scrutinized the graveclothes carefully. The Scripture uses a special word (*theoreo*) for what Peter did. The Bible says that Peter "arrived and went into the tomb. He *saw* the strips of linen lying there, as well as the burial cloth that had been around Jesus' head. The cloth was folded up by itself, separate from the linen" (John 20:6-7, italics added). At that point John entered, saw what Peter had seen, and believed in Jesus's resurrection.

That was the first moment of belief. In that moment John became the first Christian. It was not until later that the first appearances of the Lord began. Jesus appeared first to Mary Magdalene, who arrived back at the tomb after John and Peter had returned to the city. Next He appeared to the women who were then still on their way back to the city, then to Peter alone, then to the Emmaus disciples, finally, later that night, to all the disciples as they were gathered together in the upper room. All the disciples who saw the risen Lord believed. But John believed first. And he did so before he actually saw Jesus. What made him believe? What did he see that convinced him of Jesus' resurrection?

JEWISH BURIAL

It is helpful at this point to know something about the modes of Jewish burial. Every society has its distinct modes of burial, and that was true of ancient cultures as it is today. In Egypt, bodies were embalmed. In Rome and Greece they were often cremated. But in Palestine they were neither embalmed nor cremated. They were wrapped in linen bands that enclosed dry spices and placed face up, without a coffin, in tombs generally cut from the rock in the Judean and Galilean hills. Many of those tombs exist today and can be seen by any visitor to Palestine.

Another aspect of Jewish burial is of special interest for understanding John's account. In one of the most helpful books about the resurrection of Jesus ever written, a book called *The Risen Master*, published in 1901 by Henry Latham, the author called attention to a unique feature of Eastern burials that he noticed when in Constantinople during the last century. He said that the funerals he witnessed varied in many respects, depending upon whether the funeral was for a person who had been poor or for one who had been rich. But in one respect all the arrangements were identical.

Latham noticed that the bodies were wrapped in linen cloths in such a manner as to leave the face, the neck and the upper part of the shoulders bare. The upper part of the head was covered by a cloth that had been twirled about it like a turban. Latham concluded that since burial styles change slowly, particularly in the East, that mode of burial may well have been practiced in Jesus' time. He argued that it was all the more probable since the practice meshes nicely with what is told of the graveclothes in John's gospel.

There is additional evidence for that thesis. Luke tells us that when Jesus was approaching the village of Nain earlier in His ministry He met a funeral procession leaving the town. The only son of a widow had died. Luke says that when Jesus raised him from death two things happened. First, the young man sat up; that is, he was lying upon his back on the bier without a coffin. Second, he began to speak at once. Hence, the graveclothes did not cover his face. Separate coverings for the head and body were also used in the burial of Lazarus (John 11:44).

We have every reason to believe that Joseph of Arimathea and Nicodemus buried Jesus Christ in a similar manner. The body of Jesus was removed from the cross before the beginning of the Jewish Sabbath, was washed, and was wrapped in linen bands. One hundred pounds of spices were carefully inserted into the folds of the linen. Among them were aloes, an aromatic wood powdered into a fine sawdust, and myrrh, a fragrant gum that would be carefully mixed with the powder. Jesus' body was encased in the linen. His head, neck, and upper shoulders were left bare, and a linen cloth was wrapped about the upper part of His head like a turban. The body was then placed within the tomb where it lay until sometime on Saturday night or early Sunday morning.

THE RESURRECTION

What would we have seen had we been there at the moment when Jesus was raised from the dead? Would we have seen Jesus stir, open His eyes, sit up, and begin to struggle out of the bandages? Not at all! That would have been a resuscitation, not a resurrection. It would have been as if He had recovered from a swoon. Jesus would have been raised in a natural body rather than a spiritual body, which was not the case at all.

If we had been present at the moment of the resurrection, we would probably have seen one of two things: Either the body of Jesus would have seemed to disappear or it would have passed through the graveclothes and out of the sealed tomb just as it was later to pass through closed doors. John Stott says that the body was "vaporized, being transmuted into something new and different and wonderful."[1] Latham says that the body would have been "exhaled," passing "into a phase of being like that of Moses and Elias on the Mount."[2]

What would have happened then? The linen cloths would have collapsed once the body was removed because of the weight of the spices that were in them; they would have been lying undisturbed where the body of Jesus had been. The cloth which surrounded the head might well have retained its concave shape and would have lain by itself separated from the body cloths by the space where the Lord's neck and shoulders had been.

Of course, that is exactly what John says he and Peter saw when they entered the sepulchre. The eye-witness account reveals it perfectly. As John reached the tomb in the murky light of dawn he saw the graveclothes. There was something about them that attracted his attention. It was significant that they were lying there at all. John emphasized the fact, placing the word for "lying" at an emphatic position in the sentence. It might be translated: "He saw, lying there, the graveclothes" (John 20:5). Furthermore, the cloths were undisturbed. The word that John uses *(keimena)* occurs in the Greek papyrii of things that have been carefully placed in order. One document speaks of legal documents saying, "I have not yet obtained the documents, but they are lying collated." Another speaks of clothes that are "lying [in order] until you send word." Certainly John noticed that there had been no disturbance of the graveclothes.

At that point Peter arrived and went into the sepulchre. Peter saw what John had seen, but he was struck by something else. The cloth that had been around the head was not with the other clothes. It was lying in a place by itself (v. 7). What was more striking was that it had retained a circular shape. John says that it was "wrapped together." We might say that it was "twirled about itself." And there was a space between it and the clothes that had enveloped the body. When John saw that he believed.

I imagine John might have explained it like this: "Don't you see, Peter? No one has moved the body or disturbed the graveclothes. They are lying exactly as Nicodemus and Joseph of Arimathea left them on the eve of the Sabbath. Yet the

1. John R. W. Stott, *Basic Christianity* (Grand Rapids: Eerdmans Publishing Company, 1958), p. 52.
2. Henry Latham, *The Risen Master* (Cambridge: Deighton Bell, 1901), pp. 36, 54.

body is gone. It has not been stolen. It has not been moved. Clearly, it must have passed through the clothes, leaving them as we see them now. Jesus must be risen." Stott says, "A glance at these grave clothes proved the reality, and indicated the nature, of the resurrection."[3]

How foolish in the light of such evidence are the non-Christian explanations of the events of Easter morning. Some critics have taught that the body of Jesus was stolen. But in that case the presence of the graveclothes is inexplicable. They would have been removed along with the body. Others have taught that Jesus revived in the tomb and escaped after having unwound the linen bands. But in that case the linen would have been displaced. Even if we can imagine that Jesus replaced them and somehow moved the stone, there is still a problem with the spices, for they would have been scattered about the tomb. Of this there is not the slightest suggestion in the gospel. No, none of those explanations will do. The disciples saw everything in order, but the body of Jesus was gone. He had indeed been raised, and He had been raised in a resurrection body.

What John Believed

God has provided perfectly adequate evidence of the resurrection of Jesus Christ from the dead. The evidence consists of the claims of those who saw Jesus between the day of His resurrection and the day of His ascension into heaven, the empty tomb, the changed character of the disciples, the authenticity of the records, and the evidence of the undisturbed burial garments. The evidence is there, and the evidence of the graveclothes alone was sufficient to quicken faith in John. If people fail to believe, it is because they will not believe. It is not because the evidence is lacking.

God does not expect people to believe without evidence. If people do not believe, assuming they have looked at the evidence, it is because they do not want to surrender their lives to Christ and acknowledge Him as their Lord. If Jesus should return today, millions would reject Him. If He should make the claims that He made while here before, there are many who would condemn Him to death. If Jesus should rise again from the dead, there are people who would laugh and call it trickery.

At the same time, however, there are those who do believe. They have seen the evidence and have responded to it as God has enabled them by His Spirit. These are comforted to know that their faith rests not upon wishful thinking but upon the power of God and upon God's visible activity in history.

The experiences of Peter and John at the tomb indicate that the body of the Lord was glorified. It was sown a natural body and was raised a spiritual body. In that body Jesus is seated at the right hand of God where He waits in glory, interceding for His own until the moment when He will return again in judgment. Praise God

3. Stott, *Basic Christianity*, p. 55.

we need not think of Jesus today as the vulnerable Jesus of history! Jesus died, but He died once for all. He was buffeted and spit upon and cursed, but that will never be repeated.

There are people who think of Jesus as a figure hanging on a cross. Others have a mental picture of Jesus in the garden praying or wandering about doing good. But none of those pictures is completely accurate for those who live today. Paul saw the Lord on the road to Damascus, but He was not the lowly Jesus. He was the exalted Lord, surrounded by a light so bright it blinded the apostle. John saw the living Lord triumphant among the candlesticks that represent the churches. We pray today to a powerful Lord, to an exalted Lord. This Lord will return one day to take His own to be with Him in glory.

Finally, the transformation of the body of Jesus points to a new mode of life for all believers. He is the firstfruits. We, the harvest, shall be like Him in our bodies as well as in His traits of character. Our resurrection bodies will be better than our physical bodies. They will not be our physical bodies resuscitated. Our bodies hamper us. They tie us to earth, to habits, to traits of character that we have inherited from our parents. They slow our thought processes. When we are sufficiently tired they carry us away in sleep. Eventually they die.

But we are to gain by death. The resurrection body will not hamper us. The body of the risen Christ was the forerunner of our bodies, and it was and is wholly subservient to His wishes. It did not hamper Him. It freed Him. In that body He knew no pain, no suffering, no want. For us there will also be freedom. There will be no want. There will be only unlimited time and unlimited opportunities for service.

In one of his great sermons on the resurrection D. L. Moody told the story of a bright young girl about fifteen years of age who was suddenly cast upon a bed of suffering, completely paralyzed on one side and nearly blind. She could hardly see, but she could hear. As she lay in bed one day she heard the family doctor say to her parents as they stood by the bedside, "She has seen her best days, poor child." Fortunately, the girl was a believer and she quickly replied, "No, doctor, my best days are yet to come, when I shall see the King in his beauty." Her hope lay in the resurrection.

That is our hope also. The days may be bleak. Suffering may be all too real. But we look with confidence for our ultimate redemption by the power of Him who is the resurrection.

7. The Day Faith Died

There are some things that are just not possible for those of us who live in the days since the resurrection of Jesus Christ. One of them is the experience of total dismay, depression, and despair that settled in upon the disciples following the Lord's crucifixion. We know that Jesus was raised. Consequently, although we go through periods of dark disillusionment and doubt, the knowledge of the resurrection sustains us and we never despair utterly. It was not that way for the early disciples. They had been told of Christ's impending resurrection, but they had not understood it. Therefore, when Jesus died, there is a sense in which they died also.

"I WILL NOT BELIEVE"

When I speak of their death, I do not mean a literal, physical death. I mean the death of life as they knew it. For three years that mixed body of men and women had followed Jesus in his itinerant preaching ministry; and if they had faith at all, it can be said rightly that it was entirely wrapped up in Him. They did not understand much of what He said. But they tried to, and what they did understand they believed. When Jesus died their faith died also; they began to demonstrate the death of their faith by scattering back to where they had been before Jesus had called them to discipleship. The women went home. Cleopas and Mary returned to their village. The others would have returned to Galilee, for they did that anyway even after they had been convinced of Christ's resurrection. In earlier days they had given good testimonies—"You are the Christ, the Son of the living God" (Matthew 16:16), "We believe and know that you are the Holy One of God" (John 6:69)—but in the period between the crucifixion and the resurrection that had become past tense. They had believed once, but it was now over. Faith had died.

Of all those who were wrapped up in those last days before the crucifixion, none better illustrates the death of faith than Thomas, the doubting disciple. We are not told much about him, only that he was inclined to a very sober estimate of things. On one occasion, when Jesus had indicated His intention to return to the area of Jerusalem because of the sickness and death of his friend Lazarus of Bethany, Thomas had intoned grimly, "Let us also go, that we may die with him" (John 11:16). Later, in the upper room, when Jesus had declared, "You know the way to the place where I am going" (John 14:4), Thomas had countered, "Lord, we don't know where you are going, so how can we know the way?" (v. 5).

Thomas was not without faith; we would not want to say that. He probably believed as much as the others. But it was at least a rather sober faith that dealt squarely with the evidence.

In light of his character we are not at all surprised to learn that when news of the resurrection was declared to him by the disciples who had seen the resurrected Lord on the first Easter, Thomas objected: "Unless I see the nail marks in his hands and put my finger where the nails were, and put my hand into his side, I will not believe it" (John 20:25). As I read that statement I can almost hear a few more lines that were unspoken but thought: "And didn't I tell you so? Didn't I tell you it would end like this? The Lord would have been better off if he had listened to me, Thomas, rather than having stormed into the citadel of his enemies."

We call this disciple "doubting Thomas," but to speak accurately he was no doubter at that point. He was an outright unbeliever. Alexander Maclaren wrote,

> Flat, frank, dogged disbelief, and not hesitation or doubt, was his attitude. The very form in which he puts his requirement shows how he was hugging his unbelief, and how he had no idea that what he asked would ever be granted. "Unless I have so-and-so I will not," indicates an altogether [different] spiritual attitude from what "If I have so-and-so, I will," would have indicated. The one is the language of willingness to be persuaded, the other is a token of a determination to be obstinate.[1]

It was not a very commendable attitude, but so it was. So it was with all the disciples—before the resurrection.

"We Had Hoped"

It was not only faith that had died in the disciples; hope had died too. They had possessed such great hopes. Yet those had been dashed by the crucifixion.

The saddest expression of the death of hope is the statement of the Emmaus disciples recorded in Luke 24:21, though it was, of course, true of them all. Like the others, those two disciples (whom I identify as Cleopas and his wife Mary) had looked for the dawning of Messiah's reign upon earth. They thought that Jesus was that Messiah; so they had followed Him, looking for a place in that glorious messianic kingdom. Now the inconceivable had happened. He had died, and their hopes had died with Him. Their minds were so clouded by this great

---

1. Alexander Maclaren, *Expositions of Holy Scripture*, vol. 7, *Gospel of John* (Grand Rapids: Eerdmans, 1959), Part 3, p. 321.

disappointment that they did not even recognize the Lord when He drew near them on the Emmaus way. He asked them what they had been talking about and why they were sad. They answered,

> "Are you the only one living in Jerusalem who doesn't know the things that have happened there in these days?"
> "What things?" he asked.
> "About Jesus of Nazareth," they replied. "He was a prophet, powerful in word and deed before God and all the people. The chief priests and our rulers handed him over to be sentenced to death, and they crucified him; but we had hoped that he was the one who was going to redeem Israel." (Luke 24:17-21)

It is interesting that they used the word *redeemed* because, of course, that is precisely what the Lord Jesus Christ was doing—redeeming Israel and all who should thereafter believe on Him as their Savior from sin. But that is not what they were thinking. They were thinking of that national, temporal, messianic redemption upon which their hopes had been set throughout the three years of His ministry. But since Jesus had died, they knew at last that it was not coming.

The situation of those two disciples was precisely that of the others before the resurrection. Faith had died, and hope had died also.

LOVE LIVES

There was one thing that had not died. Love had not died. For in spite of their cruel disillusionment and despair, they all still loved Jesus and could not cease thinking about Him. The greatest example of that was Mary.

We do not know a great deal about this Mary, Mary of Magdalene. But we must be careful to distinguish what we do know from those spurious details that have been added to the account by years of church tradition. The Bible tells us that Mary had been the object of Christ's special grace and that He had sent seven demons out of her (Luke 8:2). For no sound reason at all, church tradition identified her with the unnamed sinner of Luke 7, who anointed the feet of Jesus in the house of a wealthy Pharisee—probably because Mary of Bethany later did the same thing in the house of Lazarus, and there was a confusion of those two accounts.

From that she was assumed to have been a prostitute before Christ saved her, and by the seventeenth century the word *Magdalene* was being used of a reformed prostitute. We do not know whether that was her case or not. But Christ had saved her from something terrible, and she had learned to love Him. Jesus said that the one who has been forgiven much, loves much (Luke 7:47). That was true of Mary. Thus, earlier in His ministry we learn that she ministered to Him out of her substance (Luke 8:3), and we find that at the end she was still trying to do that by anointing His body.

We will never understand the account of Christ's appearance to Mary at the tomb unless we recognize that it was love, only love, that brought her there. She had possessed faith once, as had the others. She had hoped. But faith and hope were gone now. Only love caused her to seek the body and stay close to the tomb.

It is a remarkable story. To begin with, Mary was one of that group of women who had been in Jerusalem at the time of the trial and crucifixion and who had therefore witnessed the Lord's agonies. We read on three separate occasions that she was among those women who saw the crucifixion (Matthew 27:55-56; Mark 15:40; John 19:25). No doubt she witnessed the other events as well—the roar of the crowd as they shouted, "Take him away! Take him away! Crucify him!"; the judgment of Pilate; the procession to Calvary, during which time Christ fell under the weight of the cross and had to be relieved of it by Simon of Cyrene in order that the death march might proceed; the driving of the nails; the terrible cries ("I am thirsty"; "My God, my God, why have you forsaken me?"); the darkness; the earthquake; at last the death. Mary witnessed all that. It would have been a severe strain on the strongest of men. Who could have the stomach for such things? Yet through it all there was Mary. What kept her there? Not curiosity, certainly. Not faith. Not hope in a miracle. Mary was there only because she loved Jesus and consequently would not leave until the end.

And even then her love lived on. For though He was gone, she still wished to do something for Him. She determined to buy spices, and the others agreed. They did so just before the shops closed for the Passover Sabbath. Sometime on that same evening they watched as the body was removed from the cross and followed it as it was hurriedly placed in Joseph of Arimathea's tomb.

The Sabbaths went by, first the Passover Sabbath (which, in that year, probably fell on a Friday) and, then, the regular Saturday Sabbath. Thus it was on the following Sunday morning that Mary and the other women—Mary the wife of Cleopas; Salome; and others—made their way to the tomb to perform their last rites. They knew that the stone had been placed over the entrance to the burial cave, for they were asking, "Who will roll the stone away from the entrance of the tomb?" (Mark 16:3). We might ask, "But then how did they expect to anoint the body?" The answer is that they did not know. They hoped that someone might be there to move the stone, but they were not really thinking clearly at that point. All they were concerned about was Jesus. They loved Him, and this was all they knew how to do.

Upon reaching the tomb they noticed in the early light of dawn that the stone had been moved. It suited their purpose, but it was not what they had been expecting. So they stopped and asked themselves what they should do. At last they decided that the disciples Peter and John should be told. Mary was either dispatched or else volunteered to tell them. While she was gone (and therefore unknown to her), the remaining women went forward, saw and heard the angel, and then rushed off in amazement to convey the angel's message: "He is not here; he has risen, just as he said" (Matthew 28:6). Shortly after they had gone Peter and John arrived, having received Mary's message and then having raced to the tomb.

And Mary? What of Mary? Well, she had been left behind by Peter and John. But that did not disturb her; her mind was on Jesus. Quite naturally she set out for the tomb once more.

I wonder if you can identify with the strain this woman was under. She had seen the person she loved most in all the world taken from her and brutally executed. She had planned to perform some last rites on the body, but that had been frustrated, at least temporarily. She had been going back and forth from the city to the tomb in the dark or semi-dark for what must have seemed hours. Now she arrived back at the tomb to find Peter and John and the other women gone. She was alone, totally deserted. It was beyond her emotional capacity. She burst out weeping. Undoubtedly she had wept before, at the crucifixion and during the days since. How she could find more tears is almost beyond understanding. But there were some. It was therefore with tear-filled eyes that she looked into the sepulchre and saw the angels.

"Woman, why are you crying?" they asked her.

She answered, "They have taken my Lord away, . . . and I don't know where they have put him" (John 20:13). Do you see the significance of this reply? Mary was not startled by the angels, as the women who preceded her were. Perhaps she did not even recognize that they were angels. All she could think about was the Lord's body. There was still no faith, no hope. But she did love Him. And now, since the body was no longer where it had been, she had no more interest either in the tomb or the angels. We read, therefore, that "at this, she turned around and saw Jesus standing there" (v. 14).

"RABBONI"

We are told that Mary did not recognize Jesus, even after He had spoken to her. Later, when He presented himself to the Emmaus disciples, they did not recognize Him either; so perhaps His appearance was changed. Besides, Mary was not seeing clearly, and she certainly did not expect the resurrection. "Woman, why are you crying? Who is it you are looking for?" (John 20:15). It was the voice of Jesus, but Mary did not recognize it. She imagined that the one speaking to her was the gardener.

Mary answered in what is surely one of the most touching sentences in all literature. "Sir, if you have carried him away, tell me where you have put him, and I will get him" (v. 15).

Donald Grey Barnhouse wrote of this poignant offer:

> She was still thinking in terms of a dead body. She had been weeping for three days and three nights, and her heart was empty even though she still had a few tears left. She had passed through unutterable anguish and had been for many hours without sleep. She had been three times out to the tomb and twice back to the town. She offered to carry away the full weight of the body of a man, plus the hundred pound weight of myrrh and aloes. The Bible tells us that the body had been anointed with one hundred

pounds of spices which Nicodemus had wrapped in the linen which enshrouded the body (John 19:39). Even if Jesus were slight of weight, Mary was offering, without thinking, to carry away a weight of body and linen cloth and ointments which would go beyond the strength of many a strong man. But she did not think of this, for she loved the Lord Jesus Christ, and though her faith and hope were dead, her love was strong. Here is one of the greatest character portrayals in all of literature, human or divine. Here is the heart of a good woman. Here is love, offering to do the impossible as love always does.[2]

At that point Mary must have turned her back on Christ, for later, after He had called her name, we read that she turned back to Him. The point is that she was not interested in the "gardener." She had made her request of Him in her grief and confusion. But her heart was still true to the Lord, and she turned back to the tomb where she had seen His body last.

"Mary."

"Rabboni [Master]!"

As Mary responded to His enunciation of her name, she turned back to Christ again. When she had supposed Him only to be the gardener, she had no interest in Him. But now her name had come to her from the lips of Jesus, and as sheep know the voice of their shepherd when he calls them by name, so did she recognize Him and respond joyfully, "Master!" In that moment Mary experienced her own resurrection; she was reborn. Faith had died, but now it came leaping from its tomb. Hope had evaporated, but now it gathered again around Jesus.

THE GREATEST OF THESE

You may be one who has never known any of these three responses to Jesus Christ—neither faith, hope, nor love. You may say that you cannot believe, that you have no grounds for hope, that you do not see how you can love Him. If this is your case, may I suggest that you begin with love. And if you say, "But how can I love?" I answer that the way to come to love Him is to begin with the knowledge that He loves you. That love is shown by His death on your behalf. Moreover, He commends His love to you by this fact. The book of Romans says, "But God demonstrates his own love for us in this: While we were still sinners, Christ died for us" (Romans 5:8).

Can you not focus on His death and love Him for that? I am convinced that if you truly focus on that death and respond to it—how can you fail to?—then the matter will not stop there. I am convinced that you will hear Him call your voice and that, when He does, you will recognize Him and gladly respond, "Master!" In that moment faith will be born in you and hope will triumph. You will be His forever.

There is an application, too, for those who already are Christians. You have

2. Donald Grey Barnhouse, "The Voice of the Risen Christ," in *First Things First* (Philadelphia: Evangelical Foundation, 1961), p. 57.

believed in Christ; you love Him. Your hope is centered in Him. But it may have happened, as it does to nearly all of us at one season or another, that tragedy has come into your life and faith and hope have both suffered from it. It may be death, perhaps that of a close friend or loved one. It may be suffering. It may even be just extremely bad news. The circumstance has confused you, and you have been wondering if you have ever really believed as you ought or if your hope for the future was ever a realistic one. If that is the case, do not despair. It has been the case of many. Instead, allow your love for Christ, which can never be destroyed by circumstances, to blossom. Draw near to Him. For when you have done so you will know that sweet communion that causes faith and hope to grow also. You will learn to keep your faith and hope moving in the same direction as your love.

Faith, hope, love! These three! "But the greatest of these is love" (1 Corinthians 13:13).

8. Why Are You Crying?

*I*t is not that Jesus was against tears or even that He "hated to see a woman cry," as we say. Earlier He had cried himself, and on the way to His crucifixion He told the weeping women who followed Him to cry for themselves and their children. One of the grandest scenes of our Lord's earthly life was His open grief at the time of His triumphal entry into Jerusalem on what we call Palm Sunday. Everyone else was rejoicing—the disciples particularly, for it was the day they had been waiting for. At last Jesus was going to take up His crown and rule in God's holy city. He was going to drive the Romans out, they thought. Instead, Jesus wept. He lamented,

> "If you, even you, had only known on this day what would bring you peace—but now it is hidden from your eyes. The days will come upon you when your enemies will build an embankment against you and encircle you and hem you in on every side. They will dash you to the ground, you and the children within your walls. They will not leave one stone on another, because you did not recognize the time of God's coming to you." (Luke 19:42-44)

Later he told the women,

> "Daughters of Jerusalem, do not weep for me; weep for yourselves and for your children. For the time will come when you will say, 'Blessed are the barren women, the wombs that never bore and the breasts that never nursed!' Then
>
> > "they will say to the mountains, 'Fall on us!'
> > and to the hills, 'Cover us!'
>
> For if men do these things when the tree is green, what will happen when it is dry?" (Luke 23:28-31)

No, it was not that Jesus was opposed to crying or that He was unduly distressed by a woman's tears. It was just that things had changed between the time of those two earlier incidents and the scene now presented to us in the garden which contained the empty tomb. Everything had changed, for He who was dead was now alive! He had risen, as He said.

A Poignant Story

On the first day of the week the women who had been in Jerusalem and had witnessed the crucifixion went to Joseph of Arimathea's tomb where they hoped to be able to anoint the body of Jesus with spices. They knew the tomb had been sealed with a stone. This was a problem. But when they arrived at the tomb and found the stone rolled away, they sent Mary Magdalene to tell Peter and John. While she was gone they went forward, saw the angels, and, at the angels' command, went off to tell the others that Jesus had risen from the dead.

Mary had not seen the angels. So when she reached Peter and John, all she really knew to tell them was that the stone had been moved. Still she assumed it had been done so that someone could move the body. She said, "They have taken the Lord out of the tomb, and we don't know where they have put him!"

Peter and John did not know either. In fact, they knew nothing. But they started for the tomb, running, and there saw the graveclothes where the body had been. This was so striking—the burial clothes could not be as they were unless Jesus had passed through them in a resurrection body, just as He was later to pass through closed doors—that John says this alone led him to belief. But neither Peter nor John saw Jesus until later. After they had seen all there was to see at the tomb they went home.

And Mary? She had been left behind in the city when Peter and John ran off. Now, having nowhere else to go and not really wanting to go anywhere else, she made her way back to the burial garden. She was crying. No wonder! She had witnessed the arrest, trial, crucifixion, and death of the one person she loved most in all the world—just days before. She was exhausted both emotionally and physically. She had been to the tomb once before, following Christ's death. That very morning she had made the journey between her home within the city and the tomb three times: once with the women, once to return and inform the two disciples, and now back to the tomb once more after everyone else had gone. It was too much for her, and even though she was a strong woman she broke down. The story says: "But Mary stood outside the tomb crying" (John 20:10).

She must have been crying a great deal, so much that the tears clouded her vision. For when she looked into the tomb, as the other women had done earlier, and saw the angels, she did not recognize that they were angels. (Nor did she recognize Jesus when in the next moment she saw Him.) The angels asked, "Woman, why are you crying?"

She said, "They have taken my Lord away, . . . and I don't know where they have put him." When she turned away from the tomb she saw Jesus standing behind her.

"Woman," He said, "why are you crying? Who is it you are looking for?"

But she thought He was the gardener and said, "Sir, if you have carried him away, tell me where you have put him, and I will get him."

Jesus spoke her name: "Mary." At once she recognized Him. Tears fled. Faith and hope revived, and she called out, "Rabboni!" which means Master or Teacher. After that her message to the others was simply, "I have seen the Lord" (John 20:15-18).

A Searching Question

"Why are you crying?" We can hardly miss the fact that in this brief story the question was asked of Mary two times, once by the angels and once by Jesus. Why? It was not because the questioners did not know the answer; they did. Anyone would have known it, and that was certainly true of Jesus, who knows everything. Nor did the angels or Jesus ask their question to tease Mary, like a person offering a piece of candy to a child but hiding it in one fist held alongside the other: "Which hand is it in?" Rather, it was to clarify her thinking and highlight the contrast between what she was looking for and the far greater blessing that was about to be given her by God.

What was Mary Magdalene looking for? The first answer to that question is that she was looking for a body, *a dead body.* What God had for her was *the living Lord.*

Nothing is more evident than that Mary was looking for a body. She was thinking of it in terms of the Jesus she loved, but she knew that He was dead and that the body was all she would have left to her, assuming she could find it. That is what the women were looking for when they made their way to the sepulchre, and Mary was of their number. These women had ministered to Jesus while He was alive. Now He was gone, but they still wanted to carry out their duties and demonstrate their love as long as possible. All they could do now was anoint the body. When she carried the women's message to Peter and John, Mary was still thinking along those lines, for her message was: "They have taken the Lord out of the tomb, and we don't know where they have put him" (John 20:2). She said the same thing to the angels later, when she had returned to the garden: "They have taken my Lord away, . . . and I don't know where they have put him" (v. 13). She expressed a similar concern to Jesus: "Sir, if you have carried him away, tell me where you have put him, and I will get him" (v. 15). Not once in all those conversations does Mary mention Jesus' name. She calls Him "the Lord" or "him," assuming that everyone will know whom she is seeking. But in spite of her fixation on Jesus and her great love for Him, not once does she think in any other terms than a body. She wants to know where *they* put *Him* so she can carry *Him* away.

In place of that dead body God had the living Jesus for her. And He was there in the garden, right beside her! He spoke her name, Mary, and she knew it was He. After that Mary never thought of a body again, for she knew that the living Jesus was her constant companion.

I do not know if we have exactly the same thing today, because our circumstances are different from Mary's. But there is a sense in which something similar happens. People look for things in religion, dead things, when what God has for them is the living Jesus. Some think that religion consists of a dead body of theology, that is, a book religion. As one whose profession requires him to read much of it, I can say that there are fewer things deader than mere book religion or book theology if Christ is not in it. It is not that theology is unimportant. It is of great importance. But theology is "the study of God," and God is the *living* God if "God" means anything. A theology without the living God and the living Christ is the deadest of all dead things. So one who has only book theology might well cry, "The theologians have taken away my Lord, and I know not where they have put Him."

Again, there is the dead body of religious forms or ritual. When we talk about ritual, we must acknowledge that it, too, is not without importance. It is a step removed from theology, since it points to theology, and is therefore less important. But it is not *un*important. If a person has good theology, a good form of religious worship is apt to follow; if he has bad theology, a bad form of worship will come from it. There can be a good theology and a good form of worship. But again, if the living Christ is not present in the worship, what are forms? They are the dead bones of faith. They comfort no one.

If you have been pursuing religious matters but have found that your heart is still empty and your soul is crying out for something you can hardly even define—for God, for reality, for beauty, for life—the problem may be that you are seeking the living among the dead, or even that you are not seeking the living God at all. What God has for you is Jesus. What Jesus asks of you is: "*Who* is it you are looking for?" Notice the "who." It is not: "*What* are you looking for?"—although that question may be important in its place. The question is rather: "*Whom* are you looking for?" You should be looking for the living Lord.

A Risen Savior

The second thing Mary was looking for was *a martyr*. He was a dead martyr, to be sure—the best martyrs always are dead—but still a martyr. In place of that, God gave Mary *a risen Savior*.

We know that Mary was looking for a martyr because of the way she talked about the nameless persons who had hounded Jesus to death. She used the word "they" when she referred to them. "They have taken the Lord out of the tomb, and we don't know where they have put him" (v. 2). "They have taken my Lord away, . . . and I don't know where they have put him" (v. 13). If you had pressed Mary, asking her whom she meant by "they," she would probably have given a very cogent answer. "They" were the religious leaders of the day whose position and prestige Jesus threatened. They had been trying to remove Jesus as a threat for some time. Everyone knew that.

If you had pressed Mary, she could have answered along that line and possibly even have given you some names. But what did that matter now? If it was not those who had conspired against Jesus, it would have been others. When Mary said "they," all she meant was that Jesus had been unfairly and unjustly treated. He had come to harm, and "they" were the cause. "They" hated Him because He was good, and He had died a martyr's death because of it.

But Jesus was no martyr! A martyr is one who dies heroically, against great odds, for his beliefs. Jesus did not die for His beliefs. He died for us. He died in our place. While living He taught what He was going to do. He said, "The Son of Man did not come to be served, but to serve, and to give his life as a ransom for many" (Mark 10:45). When instituting the Lord's Supper He maintained, "This is my blood of the covenant, which is poured out for many" (Mark 14:24; see Matthew 26:28). He spoke of Himself as living bread, saying, "This bread is my flesh, which I will give for the life of the world" (John 6:51). As the time for Him to be offered drew near we are told that Jesus steadfastly made His way to Jerusalem (Mark 10:32-34), predicting His death and resurrection as He went. Clearly Jesus saw His death, not as the death of a martyr but as that of the sacrificial lamb slain from before the foundation of the world. His death was no tragedy. It was what He had come to accomplish.

Mary had been looking for a slain hero, but God gave her a risen Savior. Henceforth, she and those who also were drawn to faith were to go into the world with a gospel of salvation from sin.

IT IS THE LORD

There was one other thing that Mary was looking for, and it is striking that she seemed to be looking for it even after the living Jesus had made Himself known to her. It was the old earthly Jesus, *a mortal,* as she supposed. Instead, God gave her *a glorified and reigning Lord.*

The story of Mary's meeting with Jesus is told with such brevity that it is necessary to add certain parts, particularly the motions of Mary, to understand it. For example, in the middle of the story John tells us that Mary saw Jesus and had the conversation with Him that we have already considered. He asked her why she was crying, and she responded that if He was the one who had taken the body away, He should tell her where it was so she could go and get it. Presumably she was looking at Him when she said this. But the next thing John tells us is that Jesus called her name, and that when He did she turned toward Him crying, "Rabboni." He does not tell us, but in order for her to have turned to Him again she must have turned away as soon as she had made her request of the one she supposed to be the gardener. She must have turned back to the tomb. That was the last place she had seen Jesus, and she was not interested in anyone else until she saw that dear body again.

There is another motion of Mary's that is important at this point. When Jesus said, "Mary," she recognized Him. She cried, "Teacher!" Then, though John does not say so, she must have rushed to Him impulsively and thrown her arms around Him for the sheer joy of having Him back again. For Jesus' next words are, "Do not hold on to me, for I have not yet returned to the Father. Go instead to my brothers and tell them, 'I am returning to my Father and your Father, to my God and your God'" (John 20:17).

Mary had expected Him to be the same old Jesus, as well she might. But although He was the same, He was different too. They had known Him "after the flesh," but now they were to know Him that way no longer. He had risen from the dead and was now to reign as Lord over the emerging church. He was giving commands, and the chief of those was to go into all the world with His gospel: "All authority in heaven and on earth has been given to me. Therefore go and make disciples of all nations, baptizing them in the name of the Father and of the Son and of the Holy Spirit, and teaching them to obey everything I have commanded you. And surely I will be with you always, to the very end of the age" (Matthew 28:18-20).

I saw an advertisement for the movie *Star Wars* which read: "May the force be with you! For two weeks only!" Jesus said, "Surely I will be with you *always*, to the very end of the age."

A Time for Tears

In the third chapter of Ecclesiastes there are words of great wisdom: "There is a time for everything, and a season for every activity under heaven: . . . a time to weep and a time to laugh, a time to mourn and a time to dance" (vv. 1, 4). Let me say emphatically, there is a time when we are to weep. We are to weep over sin, over sin's effects, over suffering, anguish, pain, and over death. We are to weep when we suffer. We are to weep when others suffer. Christianity is no stoic religion. It is not a religion of the stiff upper lip. It is a religion that recognizes sin as sin and evil as evil, and grieves for both. We will have to grieve as long as we are here in this world.

But not always! Not as those who have no hope! And not at Easter! At Easter we celebrate the resurrection of the Lord, and we rejoice with Mary, whose tears were turned to joy. How can we weep? Once we had only a dead religion, but now we have found a living person. Once we had a martyr, but now we have found a Savior. Once we had a mortal, or so we thought. Now we have a reigning Lord.

9. Walk the Emmaus Road

*I*f you are ever inclined to doubt that the Word of God continues to show life-transforming power, even in the twentieth century, you ought to read a book by England's great social critic Malcolm Muggeridge, entitled *Jesus Rediscovered*.[1] In England, and to some extent in America, Muggeridge has gained a tremendous reputation, first, as the editor of the satirical news magazine *Punch*, and then, more recently, as a television personality. As Britain's scourge of the Establishment, Muggeridge has taken on the government, the royal family, international politics, even the church. It is safe to say that in the eyes of most Englishmen there has probably never been a less likely candidate for conversion to Christ or Christianity.

Nevertheless, Muggeridge gives testimony to the power of Christ to transform his life and the lives of others. He recounts his conversion as something that happened to him when he was in Israel for the British Broadcasting System. Although several factors contributed to it, the truth of the gospel and of Christ's living presence really came to him first when, for the filming of a program on the New Testament, he was walking along the road from Jerusalem to Emmaus, as those two disciples had done nearly 2,000 years ago on the morning of Jesus' resurrection.

The road to Emmaus is a road that must be walked in one sense by everyone who would become a true Christian. It is in that light that I would like to study it. The walk started out in disbelief and sadness. It ended in joy, excitement, love, and true devotion.

CLEOPAS AND MARY

Like all Christ's appearances to the disciples after the resurrection, His appearance to the Emmaus disciples involves a story.

1. Malcolm Muggeridge, *Jesus Rediscovered* (Garden City, N.Y.: Doubleday, 1969). Muggeridge tells his personal story in the Foreword (pp. x, xi).

Who were these disciples? The answer to that question is not as uncertain as most people, who are accustomed to referring merely to the "Emmaus disciples," are likely to assume. For one thing, the story itself gives the name of one of them. Luke 24:18 says that one of the disciples was Cleopas. Moreover, if you use any good concordance of the words occurring in the New Testament and look up the word "Cleopas," you will find a second mention of his name in another account of the resurrection. The reference is John 19:25. There we read, "Near the cross of Jesus stood his mother, his mother's sister, Mary the wife of Clopas, and Mary of Magdala." It is true that John spells the name a bit differently. But the spelling of names often varied in antiquity, and here the two names undoubtedly refer to the same person. Thus, we learn that the wife of Cleopas was also present in Jerusalem at the time of the crucifixion, and we may therefore assume that she was the one returning to Emmaus with him on the morning of the resurrection.

Moreover, I believe that we can know even more than that. It seems clear to me that John has given us her name when he writes of Jesus' "mother, his mother's sister, Mary the wife of Clopas, and Mary of Magdala." I must admit that because of the way John has written this verse it is not at once obvious whether John is identifying the first Mary as the sister of the virgin Mary or as the wife of Cleopas. But a little thought shows that the second of these should be preferred.

For one thing, John seems to be distinguishing between two Marys in the second part of the verse—Mary, the wife of Cleopas, and Mary Magdalene. At least that is the most natural way of interpreting the sentence. Second, if that is not the case, then either there is an unidentified Mary in the story (making five persons) or else there is a Mary who is the sister of the virgin Mary. The first case is unlikely in itself as well as unlike John's literary style, and the second is unlikely simply because it would mean there were two sisters, both of whom were named Mary. These reasons seem to point to the wife of Cleopas being Mary, a woman who (we are told elsewhere) was also the mother of James the younger and Joses and who had been a follower of Jesus as well as a helper of Jesus and His disciples (Mark 15:40-41; see also Mark 16:1 and Luke 24:10).

The whole of the argument means that, after His appearance to Mary Magdalene in the garden early in the morning, Jesus next appeared (not counting a private, unrecorded appearance to Peter) to a man and his wife, Cleopas and Mary, and this before He appeared to any of the so-called "regular" disciples.

DISBELIEF AND SADNESS

Someone will no doubt be asking why that should have been so. But the answer is not at all mysterious. It is simply that at the time Cleopas and Mary were among the very few of Christ's disciples who knew of the crucifixion and who were therefore ready to learn about the resurrection.

We must remember that the disciples, who were last seen in the garden where

Jesus had stopped in the midst of His normal nightly return to Bethany from Jerusalem, had scattered and had no doubt returned to Bethany. The psychology of the situation demands that they would have fled away from Jerusalem, not toward it. Reason dictates that they would have hoped to collect again at the place to which they had been heading. At any rate, with the exception of Peter and John, who followed those who had arrested Jesus, none of the disciples are mentioned as being in Jerusalem until after the resurrection. They would not have traveled on the Sabbath. It is likely, therefore, that until the day of the resurrection the fact of the crucifixion was known only to Peter and John, the women who were present at the cross, including Jesus' mother, and whatever other acquaintances of Jesus were present in Jerusalem for the passover.

Here we must reconstruct what had happened. The wife of Cleopas had been present at the foot of the cross. She had seen the Lord crucified, nails driven into his hands, the cross erected. She saw the blood. She heard Him cry out. She experienced the darkness. Finally she saw the spear driven into His side. Mary would have had no doubt at all that Christ was dead. And neither would Cleopas, who may have witnessed some of those things also.

When the crucifixion was over she went home. The Passover came, and Mary and Cleopas observed it like good Jews. They waited in sadness over the holidays—from the day of the crucifixion until the day of the resurrection—for the same restraints that had kept the women from going to the sepulchre to anoint the body would also have kept Cleopas and Mary from returning home to Emmaus. The morning after the Saturday Sabbath came finally. Mary went with the other women to the tomb to anoint the body, leaving Cleopas to get their things together. She saw the angels, returned to tell Cleopas about it, and then— see how utterly remarkable this is—joined him in preparing to leave. So far from her thinking was any idea of Christ's literal resurrection!

What is more, during the time that Cleopas and Mary were getting ready to leave, the women as a body told Peter and John what they had been told by the angels. Peter and John set out for the garden sepulchre. They entered the tomb. John believed in the resurrection. Peter and John returned, told Cleopas, Mary, and the others what they had seen, and then—again it is most remarkable— Cleopas and Mary went right on packing. As soon as they were ready, they left Jerusalem. Did this Palestinian peasant couple believe in Christ's resurrection? Certainly not! Did they come to believe, as they eventually did, because of their own or someone else's wishful thinking or a hallucination? Not at all. Here was a couple who were so sad at the loss of the Lord Jesus, so miserable, so preoccupied with the reality of his death, that they would not even take twenty or thirty minutes to investigate the reports of his resurrection personally.

If someone should say, "But surely they must not have heard the reports; you are making that part of the story up," the objection is refuted by the words of Cleopas himself. For when Jesus eventually appeared to them on the road and asked why they were sad, Cleopas answered by telling Him first about the crucifixion and then adding, "In addition, some of our women amazed us. They went to the tomb early this morning but didn't find his body. They came and told us that they had seen a vision of angels, who said he was alive. Then some of our companions went to the tomb and found it just as the women had said, but him they did not see" (Luke 24:22-24).

What is it that accounts for a belief in the resurrection on the part of Christ's disciples? The answer is the resurrection itself. Nothing but the resurrection! If we cannot account for the belief of the disciples in that way, we are faced with the greatest enigma in history. If we account for it by means of a real resurrection, then Christianity is understandable.

THE ROAD TO EMMAUS

At that point Cleopas and Mary had not yet believed, and they were going home. It was over. The dream was dead, and they were sad. As they made their solitary way along the road to Emmaus Jesus came, but they did not recognize Him. The last time they had seen Him He was beaten, marred, bleeding. Here He was in a glorified body and they did not know who He was. So as they went on their way Jesus drew near them, as He does to all who walk the Emmaus road. He asked them why they were sad.

If there was ever a reply that was filled with misconceptions and misunderstandings it was this one. "Are you the only one living in Jerusalem who doesn't know the things that have happened there in these days?"

"What things?" Jesus asked.

"About Jesus of Nazareth," they replied. "He was a prophet, powerful in word and deed before God and all the people. The chief priests and our rulers handed him over to be sentenced to death, and they crucified him; but we had hoped that he was the one who was going to redeem Israel" (Luke 24:18-21).

He who should have *redeemed* Israel! Of course, that was precisely the reason for Christ's death on the cross! He was redeeming men. However, they were thinking of a different kind of redemption. Jesus Christ was redeeming them from sin, and they were thinking of a deliverance from Rome. Redemption means to buy out of slavery and to set free, and they had been hoping that Jesus would be the Messiah who should make them free as a nation and set them up with an earthly king much the way they had been under the line of David or the Maccabees. Jesus had died to redeem them from sin. But that! Oh, they did not care about that! That was not what they were looking for.

That is not what people are looking for today, either. People want freedom to pursue their own will without hindrance. We want to have our problems solved. But we do not want the problem of our sins solved quite so readily. For Christ to redeem us from sin He must condemn our sin and set us on a path of righteousness.

THREE OPENINGS

When Jesus began to open the Scriptures to Cleopas and Mary He initiated the first of three openings that are mentioned in this chapter. He opened the Scriptures; He opened their eyes; He opened their understanding. Those are so significant that they would make an outline for a study all by themselves.

The first opening takes place in the middle of the story (Luke 24:25-27), but the phrase itself occurs a bit later, in verse 32, as they reflected on what Christ had said to them: "Were not our hearts burning within us while he talked with us on the road and opened the Scriptures to us?"

Have you learned that God always works that way when He points a man or a woman to Jesus Christ? When Jesus began His ministry He went into the synagogue at Nazareth on the sabbath day and read from the sixty-first chapter of Isaiah:

> The Spirit of the Lord is on me,
> because he has anointed me
> to preach the good news to the poor.
> He has sent me to proclaim freedom for the prisoners
> and recovery of sight for the blind,
> to release the oppressed,
> to proclaim the year of the Lord's favor. (Luke 4:18-19)

When he had finished reading those words He sat down and applied them saying, "Today this scripture is fulfilled in your hearing" (v. 21). A little later the disciples of John the Baptist came to Jesus asking if He were indeed the Messiah, and once again He referred to that passage.

Where are you going to find out the truth about God? Everybody has a different idea about Him. Everybody is writing about Him. Where can you find the truth? The answer is that you will find out about God as you find out about Jesus Christ. Jesus said, "Anyone who has seen me has seen the Father" (John 14:9). You will find out about Jesus Christ only as you open the Scriptures.

The second opening is in verse 31, and it is a consequence of the first. Jesus had taught them on the way. Then, as He sat and broke bread with them in their home, "their eyes were opened and they recognized him." That is as true today as it was then. If you will open the Scriptures, God will open your eyes by his Holy Spirit, and you will recognize Jesus.

The third opening is the one we find at the very end of the story after Cleopas and Mary had returned to Jerusalem and had told the other disciples of Christ's appearance to them. We are told that as they were speaking Jesus appeared again in their midst and then "opened their minds so they could understand the Scriptures" (Luke 24:45). It was His opening of their minds that they might begin to understand in some depth the things that were written in the Old Testament concerning Him.

THREE BLESSINGS

There is a great deal more to the story of Cleopas and Mary and of their meeting with the Lord Jesus Christ. For each of those three openings had an important consequence. They should also occur for us when our Bibles, eyes, and minds are opened. When Jesus opened the Scriptures we are told that their hearts burned within them. They were saying, "Isn't this exciting? Isn't it thrilling?" And, of course, the opening of the Scriptures should be equally exciting for all who study them today. If that is not true in your life, you are not really opening the Scriptures as you ought.

There was a different consequence when Jesus opened Cleopas's and Mary's eyes. No doubt they had arrived in Emmaus toward the end of the day. They were tired. It was dark. The way to Jerusalem was difficult, long, and dangerous. Nevertheless, they experienced an immediate desire to tell others about the risen Lord. So without any great deliberation, they set out for Jerusalem the same night and there told their story. Perception of the risen Christ always leads to a testimony.

Finally, as Jesus opened their minds to understand the Scriptures, they doubtless entered into a phase of their lives in which they understood both the Scriptures and the Lord differently. Before, much of the Word of God was a mystery. Hereafter, when they would turn to the book of Genesis and read about the seed of the woman who should bruise the serpent's head, they would know that the seed was Jesus. Genesis would be new for them, and they would understand the Lord Himself better. They would read a bit further and find that He is not only the seed of the woman, He is the seed of Abraham also, the one who was to bring blessings to the nations. They would recognize the fulfilment of this prophecy in the subsequent proclamation of the gospel to the Gentiles. Cleopas and Mary would see Jesus prefigured in the life of Joseph. In Exodus He would be perceived as the Passover Lamb. In Numbers He is the rock in the wilderness from whom we receive the water of life freely. He is also the cloud who guides His people and covers them with His protection. Deuteronomy pictures Jesus Christ as the righteous one and defines that righteousness. In Joshua He is the captain of the Lord's hosts. In the psalms and prophets we are told of His suffering, death, and resurrection. In some of them—Ezekiel, Daniel, and others—we learn of His second coming in glory. The last book of the Old Testament, Malachi, portrays Jesus as the sun of righteousness risen with healing in His wings.

These three openings—the opening of the Scriptures, the opening of the eyes, and the opening of the understanding—are three great blessings that we should all desire of the resurrected Lord. When the Bible is opened and we see the Lord Jesus Christ as He is interpreted to us by the divine operation of the Holy Spirit, we will never be the same again. The Word itself will be different. It will not be a mystery. It will make sense. What is more, it will be a great blessing. For it will be the place where we meet with Jesus, who died for us and who now lives to be known by His followers.

10. *The Best News Ever Heard*

W hen World War II was ending, and General Douglas MacArthur was meeting with representatives of the Japanese government on the deck of the battleship *Missouri* in Tokyo Bay (to sign the papers that were to bring an official end to hostilities), large sectors of the world were in glad suspense. When the papers were signed, news of the event was flashed around the globe, and at once men and women everywhere went wild with joy.

I was a boy at the time. My father had been in the service for some years, and the family was then stationed at a large military base in the South. We were far from the action. But even now as I look back on the event I can remember the yelling and shouting that took place when news of the end of the war finally came. In those hours parties began which went on for days.

The end of World War II was great news. Yet, great as that news was, it does not compare with the truly stupendous news of the resurrection of Jesus Christ. That was the best news this world has ever heard.

UNSHAKABLE EVIDENCE

Why? Why is the resurrection of Jesus Christ the best news the world has ever heard? The answers are simple: it is true; it came after an apparent defeat; it proves many important things; and finally, it calls for a life-saving response from each of us.

First, the resurrection of Jesus Christ is good news because *it is true*. It is possible to have reports of events that sound like good news but later prove to be disappointments because the facts of the reports are wrong or because the events did not actually happen. To use my former illustration, similar disappointments actually happened several times prior to the actual end of World War II. False reports of an end to the war spread, but they were eventually proved false and so

77

were terribly disappointing. That was not the case with news of the resurrection of the Lord.

The first great evidence for the resurrection of Jesus Christ is the evidence of the narratives themselves. These stand up to the most stringent of critical scrutinies. To begin with, there are four independent accounts. These were not made up in collusion, for if they were, they would not possess the number of apparent contradictions they contain: the number of angels at the tomb, the number of women who went to the garden, the time of their arrival, and other points. These accounts can be harmonized, but the point is that those apparent discrepancies would have been eliminated if the writers had got together to make up a stor . On the other hand, it is also apparent that they did not make the stories up separately because, if they had done that, there would never have been the large measure of overriding agreement they possess. Thus, the setting and the characters are the same, the sequence of events makes sense, and so on. Well, then, if the accounts were not made up in collusion and if they were not made up separately, the only remaining possibility is that they were not made up at all. That is, they are simply four true and independent accounts by those who knew what they were writing.

Next there is the evidence of the empty tomb, coupled with the evidence of the moved stone and the undisturbed graveclothes. How are we to account for those things? Some have imagined that either Joseph of Arimathea or the Roman or Jewish authorities moved the body. But not only was there no reason for that to have been done—it would have involved violating the officially sealed tomb—it is also inconceivable that the true circumstances would not have been revealed later after the disciples had appeared in Jerusalem to proclaim their belief in Christ's resurrection. It would have been easy to produce a body, had there been one. On the other hand, the disciples did not steal the body of Jesus, for they would hardly have been willing to die (as most of them later did) for such an illusion.

It is also possible to add the changed character of these men as evidence, for whatever happened turned them from disillusioned cowards to mighty proclaimers of the Christian message.

Then, too, we must add the appearances of Jesus, not just to one or two women in a garden under somewhat eerie circumstances, but to a wide variety of people in a wide variety of circumstances. Paul lists some of those appearances in 1 Corinthians, noting that at one point Jesus appeared even to five hundred believers at one time (1 Corinthians 15:6).

One of the greatest evidences of the resurrection is the unnatural change of the Christian day of worship from Saturday, the Jewish day of worship, to Sunday. Nothing but the resurrection of Jesus on the first day of the week explains it.

What are we to say about the force of these evidences? It is not at all overstating the case to say, as Thomas Arnold once did, that "the resurrection of Jesus Christ is the best attested fact in history." Lawyers in particular have found this to be true. In fact, some of the best books on the resurrection have been written by lawyers, some of whom originally set out to disprove the miracle. I am thinking of Frank Morison, Gilbert West, J. N. D. Anderson, and others. Sir Edward Clark, another English jurist, once wrote:

> As a lawyer I have made a prolonged study of the evidences for the first Easter day. To me the evidence is conclusive, and over and over again in the High Court I secured the verdict on evidence not nearly so compelling. As a lawyer I accept the gospel evidence unreservedly as the testimony of men to facts that were able to substantiate it.[1]

That is why the resurrection of Jesus Christ is good news. It is good news, not because it is a nice story which gives us an opportunity for a holiday once a year, but because it is true. As truth it is one of the most amazing and important facts in history.

"Wellington Defeated"

Second, the resurrection of Jesus Christ is good news because *it came after an apparent defeat*. A victory is always good news. But news of victory after news of apparent defeat is even better.

Let me illustrate that by the way in which news of the battle of Waterloo first came to England. There was no fast electronic communication in those days, but everyone knew that a great battle was pending. They were anxious to hear what would happen when Wellington, the British general, faced Napoleon. A signalman was placed on the top of Winchester Cathedral with instructions to keep his eye on the sea. When he received a message, he was to pass the message on to another man on a hill. That man was to pass it on to another. So it was to go until news of the battle was finally relayed to London and then across England. At length a ship was sighted through the fog which on that day lay thick on the channel. The signalman on board sent the first word—*Wellington*. The next word was *defeated*. Then fog closed in and the ship could no longer be seen. "Wellington defeated!" The message was sent across England, and great gloom descended over the countryside. After a few hours the fog lifted, and the signal came again— *"Wellington defeated the enemy!"* Now England rejoiced.

When Jesus died, His friends plunged into sadness. It was an apparent defeat. But, then, on the third day He rose again. When Jesus died men might have cried, "Christ is defeated, evil has triumphed, sin has won." But after three days the fog lifted, and the message came through to this world: "Jesus has risen; Jesus has defeated the enemy."

Essential Doctrines

Third, the resurrection of Jesus Christ is good news because *it proves many important things*. It proves all that needs to be proved: the essential doctrines of Christianity.

---

1. Quoted by Michael Green, *The Day Death Died* (Downers Grove, Illinois: InterVarsity, 1982), pp. 45-46.

First, it proves that there is a God and that the God of the Bible is the true God. Reuben A. Torrey, who often spoke and wrote well on these themes, put it this way:

> Every effect must have an adequate cause, . . . and the only cause adequate to account for the resurrection of Christ is God, the God of the Bible. While here on earth, as everyone who has carefully read the story of his life knows, our Lord Jesus went up and down the land proclaiming God, the God of the Bible, "the God of Abraham, Isaac and Jacob" as he loved to call him, the God of the Old Testament as well as the New. He said that men would put him to death, that they would put him to death by crucifixion, and he gave many details as to what the manner of his death would be. He further said that after his body had been in the grave three days and three nights, God, the God of Abraham, the God of Isaac and the God of Jacob, the God of the Bible, the God of the Old Testament as well as the God of the New Testament, would raise him from the dead. This was a great claim to make. It was an apparently impossible claim. For centuries men had come and men had gone, men had lived and men had died, and as far as human knowledge founded upon definite observation and experience was concerned, that was the end of them. But this man Jesus does not hesitate to claim that his experience will be directly contrary to the uniform experience of long, long centuries. . . .
>
> That was certainly an acid test of the existence of the God he preached, and his God stood the test. He did exactly the apparently impossible thing that our Lord Jesus said he would do. . . . The fact that Jesus was thus miraculously raised makes it certain that the God who did it really exists and that the God he preached is the true God.[2]

Second, the resurrection of Jesus Christ proves the deity of our Lord. When He lived upon earth Jesus claimed to be equal to God and that God, that same God, would raise Him from the dead three days after His execution by the Roman authorities. If He was wrong in that, His claim was either the raving of a deranged man or blasphemy. If He was right, the resurrection would be God's way of substantiating the claim. Did He substantiate it? Did Jesus rise from the dead? Yes, He did! The resurrection is God's seal on Christ's claim to divinity. This is why Paul, who knew that Jesus had been raised, writes that Jesus was "declared with power to be the Son of God by his resurrection from the dead" (Romans 1:4).

That is good news. If Jesus Christ is God, then God is like Jesus Christ. It means that God is not distant, arbitrary, or unreal. He is a God who loves you and came to be a ransom for your sins. We see this through the cross and resurrection.

Then, too, the resurrection proves that all who believe in Jesus Christ are justified before God. Paul teaches that in Romans also, for he states that Jesus "was delivered over to death for our sins and was raised to life for our justification" (Romans 4:25). How does that happen? Well, Jesus claimed that His death would atone for man's sin. He said that He had come "to give [his] life as a ransom for many" (Matthew 20:28). He died as He said. But the question still remained: Could it be true that the death of this man would be acceptable to God for others?

2. R. A. Torrey, *The Uplifted Christ* (Grand Rapids: Zondervan, 1965), pp. 70-71.

Suppose He had sinned? In that case, He would have been dying for His own sin rather than the sins of others. Did He sin or was His atonement valid? Three days passed. Christ arose. Thus, His claim was established. God has shown by the resurrection that Christ was sinless and that He has accepted His Son's atonement.

Torrey wrote on this point:

> When Jesus died, he died as my representative, and I died in him; when he arose, he arose as my representative, and I arose in him; when he ascended up on high and took his place at the right hand of the Father in the glory, he ascended as my representative, and I ascended in him; and today I am seated in Christ with God in the heavenlies. I look at the cross of Christ, and I know that atonement has been made for my sins; I look at the open sepulcher and the risen and ascended Lord, and I know the atonement has been accepted. There no longer remains a single sin on me, no matter how many or how great my sins may have been.[3]

The resurrection of Jesus Christ also proves that the believer in Christ can have a supernatural victory over sin in this life, for Jesus lives to provide the supernatural power to do it. This is an argument developed in the sixth chapter of Romans. In the opening verses of that chapter Paul writes, "We were therefore buried with him through baptism into death in order that, just as Christ was raised from the dead through the glory of the Father, we too may live a new life" (Romans 6:4). This means that by faith all who believe in Christ are united to Christ so that His power becomes available to them. We may be weak and utterly helpless, unable to resist temptation for a single minute. But He is strong, and He lives to give help and deliverance every moment. Victory is not a question of my strength, but of His power. His power is what I need.

Torrey, whom I have just quoted, tells a story that illustrates that point. Four men were once climbing up the most difficult face of the Matterhorn. There was a guide, a tourist, a second guide, and a second tourist, all roped together. As they went over a particularly difficult place, the lower tourist lost his footing and went over the side. The sudden pull on the rope carried the lower guide with him, and he carried the other tourist along also. Three men were now dangling over the cliff. But the guide who was in the lead, feeling the first pull upon the rope, drove his ax into the ice, braced his feet, and held fast. The first tourist then regained his footing, the guide regained his, and the lower tourist followed. They then went on in safety.

So it is in this life. As the human race ascended the icy cliffs of life, the first Adam lost his footing and tumbled headlong over the abyss. He pulled the next man after him, and the next, and the next, until the whole race hung in deadly peril. But the second Adam, the Lord Jesus Christ, kept His footing. He stood

3. R. A. Torrey, *The Bible and Its Christ: Being Noonday Talks with Business Men on Faith and Unbelief* (New York: Revell, 1904-1906), pp. 107-8.

fast. All who are united to Him by a living faith are secure and can regain the path.

Finally, the resurrection of Jesus Christ is also evidence for our own resurrection and of a life with Jesus in glory beyond the grave. Jesus said, when He was here on earth, "In my Father's house are many rooms; if it were not so, I would have told you. I am going there to prepare a place for you. And if I go and prepare a place for you, I will come back and take you to be with me that you also may be where I am" (John 14:2-3). He is preparing that place now. Can we trust Him? Was He telling the truth? If the resurrection vindicates His other sayings, it vindicates these as well; and the Christian, you and I who believe in Him, can receive them with confidence. The end of this life is not a question mark—it is Jesus. We shall be with Him.

"COME AND LEARN"

I have given three good reasons to show that the resurrection of Jesus Christ is the best news this world ever heard: (1) it is true; (2) it came after an apparent defeat; (3) it proves many important things. But there is a fourth reason also. The resurrection of Jesus Christ is good news because *it calls for a life-saving response in faith from each of us.* Have you responded in faith to this one who died for you and rose again on that far-off, first Easter morning?

There is some news that is by its very nature restricted. It applies to one or two individuals, but not to everybody. A promotion is good news to the man who receives it but not to the two or three others who failed to get the job. The results of an election are good news to the winning party but not to the losing party. Even the report of a reduction in federal income taxes is good news only to those who pay taxes or who live in the country where the reduction is to take place. Almost all human news is restricted. But the good news of the resurrection is for all.

Have you heard the good news? Have you believed it? Have you trusted in the risen Lord? This is the heart of Christianity. It is not found in the liturgies of the churches, nor in the specific formulations of Christian theology, important as they may be. Christianity is Christ, the risen Christ. He died and rose again for you. Will you not come to Him?

11. *Jesus and the Resurrection*

We can usually identify with the Bible's portrayal of events and characters because they are so real. That should be true of Paul's trip to Athens.

The visit took place in the course of Paul's second missionary journey. Paul was tired. Shortly before that, Paul and his companions, Silas and Timothy, heard the Macedonian call and passed over into northern Greece from Asia. There they ministered together. But on the way down the coast Silas and Timothy were left behind to work at Berea, and Paul traveled on to Athens alone. Apparently he intended merely to wait in Athens for his fellow-workers. But as Paul waited he was increasingly distressed by the city's idolatry. He began to speak about it and was eventually invited to address the court of the Areopagus, which he did in the sermon recorded in Acts 17. We are told by Luke that he was preaching "the good news about Jesus and the resurrection" (v. 18).

If any incident in the long and varied life of the apostle Paul parallels our own circumstances as Christians in America in this century, it is that one. The culture of Athens had passed its peak at that period of history, as many would say ours has. It had entered a long afternoon of decline and was given, not to the vigorous mental and artistic excellence that had marked the great Golden Age of Pericles but to vain talk about the latest news or curiosity. Athens was religiously superstitious but at the same time strangely secular, as our society is. Athens was materialistic. Against this came one man—a renegade rabbi who believed that the decisive work of God had recently taken place in the life, death, and resurrection of an itinerant Jewish preacher, Jesus of Nazareth, and who believed that this gospel alone could change the world.

We are like Paul. We are tired. We feel alone against the weight of history. But as Paul was stirred, so would I be and so would I have you be. For our world, no less than Athens, needs this gospel.

PROCLAIMING GOD

The word *Areopagus* does not refer, as some earlier translations have it, to a place—the Hill of Mars opposite the Acropolis—but to a council of the leading men of Athens. It was before this council that Paul spoke. These men were entrusted with knowing what was being taught in the city and with regulating that teaching. When Paul preached Jesus, some thought him to be a vain "babbler." They used a word which Aristophanes had used to describe a bird picking up seeds. It meant a dabbler in philosophy, one who has no clearly defined system—that is, not a Stoic or an Epicurean (the systems then prominent in Athens). Others perceived Paul to be advocating "foreign gods." Unlike the first, that was a serious assessment; it was the charge for which Socrates had been executed. It is no surprise, then, that Paul was cited to give an account of his teachings before this body.

"Men of Athens!" he said, addressing the most educated men of his day. "I see that in every way you are very religious. For as I walked around and observed your objects of worship, I even found an altar with this inscription: TO AN UNKNOWN GOD. Now what you worship as something unknown I am going to proclaim to you" (Acts 17:22-23).

That brings us to the first of Paul's points. The initial message that Paul had for Athens was the nature of God. When I say that I do not mean to imply that it is sufficient or even possible to have a correct view of God without Christ. Paul did not teach that. One aspect of his teaching about God in this very sermon is His holiness expressed in the matter of judgment; but that is known only through the death and resurrection of Jesus. Indeed, as Paul would have gone on to show, the only true knowledge of God in any aspect is through His self-revelation in Christ. Still, many false ideas about God need to be stripped away in order that the God who is now revealed in Jesus might be seen clearly. That is what I mean when I say we must begin with God.

It was as though Paul was clearing away a lot in order to construct a house. He was going to build the fine house of revealed religion. But the lot on which he was building, Athens, was already occupied by the shanty town of the various Greek religions, and Paul needed to pull those down so he could build permanently to God's glory.

In those days nothing was more characteristic of Athens than its temples. Possibly the most outwardly religious city in the world at that time, Athens had erected temples and provided homes not only for the vast pantheon of Greek gods but literally for all known gods both of the Roman West and the Orient. One commentator writes,

> Nearly every public building was actually a shrine—the Record House, for example, was a temple to the mother of gods, the Council House housed statues to Apollo and Jupiter, the theater at the foot of the Acropolis was consecrated to Bacchus. The magnificent Acropolis itself, the focal point of Athens, was actually a vast and ornate

collection of sanctuaries. Everywhere in the city there were shrines and temples, each with carved statuary, each an architectural masterpiece. There were altars dedicated even to abstractions such as Fame, Energy, Modesty, and Persuasion. Some altars had been erected years before when, during a plague, Epimenides had brought in a flock of black and white sheep, and had ordered a sacrifice and altar on the place wherever a sheep lay down.[1]

In at least one case, according to Paul's observation, there was an altar "to an unknown god." Due to this proliferation of altars, a Greek philosopher had said some years before Paul's arrival that "in Athens it is easier to find a god than a man."

But for all those gods there was nevertheless a numbing sameness about the city. The reason was that, for all their artistic grace and visual variety, the statue gods were made by and for man. So in worshiping the God who was unknown to them, the Greeks had merely invented gods in man's image, regardless of the name or names by which they were called.

Moreover, Greeks had tired of their gods and goddesses—at least as true gods and goddesses—for philosophy had become increasingly materialistic. The Epicureans regarded matter as all there is, though Epicurus himself (341 to 270 B.C.) did not deny the existence of the gods. He simply denied their interference in human life. Epicureans believed that pleasure was the chief end of life. The Stoics, who regarded Zeno (c. 300 B.C.) as their founder, were pantheists and rationalists. They believed in conformity to nature, exhibiting a rigid self-control and maintaining extreme self-sufficiency. The Stoic spirit could have been expressed in the well-known lines from Henley's poem "Invictus":

> I am the Master of my fate;
> I am the Captain of my soul.

In that age the Greek was outwardly religious but inwardly a materialist who regarded himself as his own god.

That is a description of our age also, and that is why Paul's proclamation of the true God is equally necessary for our time. It is true that in this address Paul did not have opportunity to develop the doctrines of God as fully as he did elsewhere, in the epistle to the Romans, for example. But he said enough. He proclaimed God as the Creator of heaven and earth, a doctrine taught as far back as the opening verse of Genesis but denied by all branches of Greek philosophy, which generally regarded matter as eternal. He spoke of God's benevolent nature, for all that we have—"life and breath and everything else"—is from Him. He spoke of God's providence, showing that He determines the duration of a man's or woman's life and fixes the places where people and the nations they constitute should live.

1. William P. Barker, *They Stood Boldly: Men and Women in the Book of Acts* (Westwood, New Jersey: Revell, 1967), pp. 136-37.

Moreover, said Paul, He did this "so that men would seek him and perhaps reach out for him and find him" (Acts 17:27). Although Paul did not develop it here, we know from other portions of his writings that no one has responded to God's benevolence by seeking after Him. Sin is the problem. In fact, it causes people to run from God, and it is why the judgment of God, mentioned toward the end of Paul's sermon, is necessary.

Here, then, is a sovereign, benevolent, but judging God—the very God people need to know about but refuse to acknowledge. He is the God the Athenians were ignorant of, but whom Christianity proclaims. He is what we proclaim, if we are faithful to our Master's instructions.

THE FAILURE OF RELIGION

The second point of Paul's message to the Athenians is the failure of religion. That is mingled among Paul's other points, but it is obvious from the address itself and from the context in which Luke so adroitly places it. The purpose of religion is to seek out and know God. If religion fails to help people find and know God, it fails as religion, whatever else it may or may not accomplish. That is precisely what the religions of Paul's day and the religions of our day are guilty of. They talk big, but they do not assist the worshiper to know God.

Luke indicates this in a subtle contrast between the words *know* (repeated twice on the lips of the religious philosophers, vv. 19, 20) and *unknown* (which occurs twice in Paul's sermon, v. 23). The philosophers made great claims to knowledge. When they brought Paul before the assembly of the Areopagus they said, "May we *know* what this new teaching is that you are presenting? You are bringing some strange ideas to our ears, and we want to *know* what they mean." To *know* was their business. But Paul began his speech with a contrast between this alleged knowledge and the fact that the true God actually was *unknown* to them: "What you worship as something unknown I am going to proclaim to you."

Moreover, there is this additional irony. Not only did the philosophers not know God, they did not know and could not even agree on what Paul was teaching. At the beginning some said that he was only a babbler, but others a proclaimer of strange gods; at the end they were in similar disarray (vv. 32-34).

JESUS AND THE RESURRECTION

No doubt the philosophers would have argued strenuously for their own positions. But their arguments were meaningless in religious matters because the true God was unknown to them. In all that company there was only one man who knew what he was talking about. That was Paul. And he knew, not because he was a better educated or shrewder philosopher than the others (though he was certainly shrewd and well-educated), but because his views were based upon the revelation of God in history in the person of Jesus of Nazareth, whom God raised from the dead. If Paul had been allowed to finish, he would certainly have said a great deal more about Jesus. In fact, he had prepared for it. When he argued that "we are God's offspring" and should therefore not think "that the divine being is like gold or silver or stone—an image made by man's design and skill" he was undoubtedly preparing to teach about the incarnation. He was going to say that the way we should expect God to reveal Himself to us is as a man. Moreover, when he contrasts "the past" with the present ("now"), he is bracketing that decisive period when Jesus "died for our sins according to the Scriptures, . . . was buried, . . . was raised on the third day according to the Scriptures," and was afterward seen by many witnesses (1 Corinthians 15:3-8).

Paul's actual teaching was,

> Therefore since we are God's offspring, we should not think that the divine being is like gold or silver or stone—an image made by man's design and skill. In the past God overlooked such ignorance, but now he commands all people everywhere to repent. For he has set a day when he will judge the world with justice by the man he has appointed. He has given proof of this to all men by raising him from the dead (Acts 17:29-31).

Thus, Paul returned to his original message: Jesus and the resurrection.

We know the result of that preaching. Apparently, so many regarded teaching about a resurrection absurd that Paul had to break off and shortly after even left Athens. But truth is not to be judged by how many scorn or do not scorn it, but by the evidence for or against that truth. That is what Paul had and what the philosophers of Athens lacked. Indeed, that is what set Paul's gospel off from anything any of these others might have thought up. His gospel was grounded in the facts of history.

In the early part of this century, in the heyday of modernism in American religion, it was customary to trace the origin of Paul's religion to pre-Christian apocalyptic notions of the Messiah or myths of paganism. But in 1925, J. Gresham Machen published a book in which he demolished those modernistic theories forever. In fact, he did for them much as he had done for the theories of those who traced the origins of belief in the virgin birth to pre-Christian Jewish or pagan sources (in *The Virgin Birth of Christ*, 1930). The book on Paul is entitled *The Origin of Paul's Religion*. It concludes with this summary:

> Here lies the profoundest of all differences between Paul and contemporary religion. Paulinism was not a philosophy; it was not a set of directions for escape from the misery of the world; it was not an account of what had always been true. On the contrary, it was an account of something that had happened. The thing that had happened, moreover, was not hidden in the dim and distant past. The account of it was not evolved as a justification for existing religious forms. On the contrary, the death and resurrection of Jesus, upon which Paul's gospel was based, had happened only a few years before. And the facts could be established by adequate testimony; the eyewitnesses could be questioned, and Paul appeals to the eyewitnesses in detail. The single passage, 1 Corinthians 15:1-8, is sufficient to place a stupendous gulf between the Pauline Christ and the pagan savior-gods. But the character of Paulinism does not

depend upon one passage. Everywhere in the epistles Paul stakes all his life upon the truth of what he says about the death and resurrection of Jesus. The gospel which Paul preached was an account of something that had happened. If the account was true, the origin of Paulinism is explained; if it was not true, the Church is based upon an inexplicable error.[2]

What had happened? God had sent His Son, Jesus of Nazareth, to reveal His true person and nature and then to die for human sin. Moreover, He had then raised Him from the dead as proof that Jesus was who He claimed to be, was true in what He taught, and did make an acceptable atonement for our sins by His self-sacrifice. Besides, He also lives to be loved and served by those who have come afterward.

Machen concludes:

> The religion of Paul was not founded upon a complex of ideas derived from Judaism or from paganism. It was founded upon the historical Jesus. But the historical Jesus upon whom it was founded was not the Jesus of modern reconstruction, but the Jesus of the whole New Testament and of Christian faith; not a teacher who survived only in the memory of his disciples, but the Savior who after his redeeming work was done still lived and could still be loved.[3]

That was the religion Paul preached and that needs to be preached today. Our world is equally ignorant. This religion needs to be preached by a generation of those who, like Paul, truly know and love the Lord Jesus Christ and who have a faith that is grounded in the facts of history, as his was.

THE SEQUEL

It is possible that Paul was disappointed with his evangelistic work in Athens, for he seems to have made a shift in approach after going on to Corinth: "When I came to you, brothers, I did not come with eloquence or superior wisdom as I proclaimed to you the testimony about God. For I resolved to know nothing while I was with you except Jesus Christ and him crucified" (1 Corinthians 2:1-2). If this is a real shift, it may be because there was no great response to the gospel. No church was established.

Yet, although there was no *great* response to Paul's preaching in Athens, nevertheless there was some. Later, in writing to the Corinthians, Paul says, "Not many of you were wise by human standards; not many were influential; not many were of noble birth" (1 Corinthians 1:26). But "many" is not "any," and in Athens even among the wisest and noblest of the ancient world there were some who were blessed by God in being given ears to hear and who therefore responded by believing in Jesus. Some "sneered." Some postponed their decision ("We want to

2. J. Gresham Machen, *The Origin of Paul's Religion* (Grand Rapids: Eerdmans, 1947), pp. 316-17.
3. Ibid.

hear you again on this subject"). But some believed, among whom was Dionysius, a member of the very council before whom Paul spoke ("a member of the Areopagus"), a woman named Damaris, and some others.

If you have not yet believed in Jesus, I challenge you to join their number. _I challenge_. But _God commands_. Paul says, "Now he commands all people everywhere to repent. For he has set a day when he will judge the world with justice by the man he has appointed. He has given proof of this to all men by raising him from the dead" (Acts 17:30).

12. *Preaching the Resurrection*

The doctrine of the resurrection is so important and is treated so thoroughly in 1 Corinthians 15 that the chapter invites comparison with Hebrews 11, the great chapter on faith, on the one hand, and 1 Corinthians 13, the great chapter on love, on the other. At the very end of 1 Corinthians 13 Paul pulls these themes together, saying, "Now these three remain: faith, hope and love" (v. 13). Since the resurrection is the essence of the Christian hope, he is actually addressing the three themes covered in these chapters. The resurrection is one of the three key doctrines of Christianity.

First Corinthians 15 is a long chapter—fifty-eight verses. Yet the outline is simple. In the first section (vv. 1-11), Paul talks about the *truth* of the resurrection. The second section (vv. 12-34) deals with the *importance* of the resurrection. In the third section (vv. 35-49), the apostle remarks (in the nature of an aside) about the resurrection *body*. He is handling objections. Finally (vv. 50-58), Paul considers the *victory* which is ours through the resurrection and the accompanying defeat of death. His conclusion is that we are to stand firm, unmoved, and abound always in God's work.

RESURRECTION TRUTH

It is evident in verses 1-11 that Paul is thinking about the whole of the gospel and about the role the resurrection had in the gospel message from the beginning. He was aware, both as he wrote here and often elsewhere, that he had come along relatively late as an apostle. He was a true apostle; he had received a commissioning to be an ambassador to the Gentiles. But he had not been among the twelve, and therefore he had not lived with the Lord during the days of His earthly ministry. He had not witnessed the crucifixion or resurrection. Because of this, it might be supposed—perhaps this is what his critics said—that Paul did not know the true gospel and had instead somehow along the way developed a theology of his own, including this "speculation" about the resurrection.

Paul says here that this was not the case. On the contrary, the gospel which he proclaimed to others was something he had first received himself. He received it from the earliest witnesses. Therefore, what he preached and what they preached was one identical gospel, namely, "that Christ died for our sins according to the Scriptures, . . . [and] that he was raised on the third day according to the Scriptures" (vv. 3-4).

This is very important, for it means that Paul had not invented his theology. What he passed on through 1 Corinthians 15 and other writings is not something that was concocted by Christian theologians in the early days of church history or something that grew out of the sanctified spiritual experience of the church—as is said to have happened by certain German theologians today. Rather it is what was preached in the church from the very beginning, because it was known from the beginning. It was based upon fact, namely, that Jesus lived, died, was buried and rose again, all in accordance with the Scriptures. Jesus' life and work were in accord with the previously announced plan of God.

So when we talk about the Christian faith we are not talking primarily about a philosophy, though Christianity has philosophical overtones. We are not talking about a system of morality, though Christianity has moral implications. We are talking about truth—something that has occurred in history and that makes all the difference in the world.

When we discuss the resurrection today, it is customary to deal with the evidences for the resurrection. There are many. First, there is the evidence of the narratives themselves—the four gospels—which tell of the resurrection. When we subject these stories to careful analysis it is evident that they are not invented stories. There are only two ways in which they could be made up, and neither fits what we know of them. Either they would have to have been invented in isolation from one another, or they would have to have been invented in collusion with one another. If they had been made up in isolation from one another, they would differ so widely that they would not even tell the same story. That is not the situation. Anybody, whether he or she is a Christian or not, can recognize that the gospels are telling the same story about the same people set in the same period. Yet they were not made up in collusion either, as if Matthew, Mark, Luke, and John got together and said, "Let's write a story about Jesus' supposed resurrection." If they had done that, the gospels would not have the kind of small variations they have. We can harmonize these details by careful comparison. They are even what we would expect from eye-witness testimony. But if the writers were inventing the story, this is precisely the type of variation they would eliminate. For example, they would not allow one writer to say that there was one woman who went to the tomb and another writer to say that a group of women went to the tomb. They would notice the apparent contradiction and resolve it one way or another.

What is the conclusion? Well, if the resurrection accounts were not made up independently of one another, and if they were not fabricated in collusion, the obvious and inevitable conclusion is that they are genuine. In other words, they are what they purport to be, namely, men testifying to what they knew to be true through personal experience.

A second line of evidence deals with the empty tomb. The body was gone. Nothing is clearer than that. Where did it go if there was no resurrection? Did the enemies of Jesus steal it? Did they say, "The disciples are going to take Jesus' body and hide it. They are going to say that there has been a resurrection. Let's take it first. Then, when they begin their preaching, at least we'll know where the body is." If that had been the case, it is inexplicable that the enemies of Christ did not produce the body when the disciples started to proclaim the resurrection. If they wanted to extinguish this claim, the easiest thing in the world would have been to say, "Christianity is utterly unfounded because the body of Jesus is still with us. Look! Here it is!" That would have nipped Christianity in the bud. If the enemies of Jesus did not produce the body, it was because they did not have it. You say, "Well, maybe the disciples took it. Maybe they hid it so they could proclaim a resurrection." If that were the case, is it conceivable that these men—Peter, John, James, and the others—would later have died, as they did, for what they knew to be a complete fabrication? People do not sacrifice themselves for myths. If the enemies of Jesus did not take the body, and the friends of Jesus did not take the body, the body was not taken. The body of Jesus was raised from the tomb as Jesus said it would be.

Third, there is the evidence of the graveclothes. They were left behind. Moreover, they were not scattered about the tomb, as one might expect if somebody had unwrapped them in order to cart away the naked body. They were exactly as they had been when they were around the body. The linen bands were where the body had been. The head cloth was where the head had been. How was one to account for that? The only explanation is that the body passed through the graveclothes, just as it was later to pass through closed doors.

Fourth, we have the changed lives of the disciples. They had been cowardly. Like Peter, they were afraid to confess their Lord publicly. Afterward they were transformed, so much so that they stood in the very city where Jesus had been crucified and proclaimed to the people who had been instrumental in His crucifixion: "This man was handed over to you by God's set purpose and fore-knowledge; and you, with the help of wicked men, put him to death by nailing him to the cross. But God raised him from the dead" (Acts 2:23-24). Nothing but a miracle produces change like that.

One of my favorite evidences for the resurrection is the change of the Christian day of worship from the sabbath (Saturday), the day Jews observed, to Sunday, the first day of the week. The early Christians were Jews. Jews worshiped on the seventh day, because this was the day God had chosen for Him to be worshiped: "The seventh day is a Sabbath to the Lord your God" (Exodus 20:10). Yet without any discussion, apparently without any argument at all, the worship habits of the church were suddenly switched over from the seventh day of the week to the first. Why? Obviously, because the early Christians believed that Jesus had been raised from the dead on the first day of the week and met, not to observe the old traditions of Judaism, but to mark the resurrection.

These are all great, mighty, powerful historical evidences of Jesus' resurrection. Yet as we read 1 Corinthians 15 we do not find Paul talking about any of them. Instead he is talking about those who had *seen* the risen Lord. This is because, if Peter, then the twelve, then up to five hundred people at one time, then James, then all the apostles and last of all Paul, had seen Him, in a certain sense any other arguments for the resurrection were irrelevant. The testimony of these many and diverse individuals was so beyond the possibility of falsification that they alone were overwhelming evidence to its historicity.

I repeat what I suggested earlier. Christianity, unlike many of the religions of the world, is not a religion of ideas, primarily. We like ideas. Take a university course in religion, and you will find that it is filled with ideas. You will study the ideas present in all types of religions. You will be free to pick the ones that seem most satisfying to you. This is not the way with Christianity. Christianity concerns historical truth. So, whether you like it or not, whether it appeals to you or not, this, according to Christianity, is what happened: Jesus died, was buried (which means that He was really dead), and then rose again from the dead, all according to the Scriptures.

THE IMPORTANCE OF THE RESURRECTION

Someone might say, "But who cares if the resurrection is true? I won't argue with it. Truth can be truth. The resurrection just doesn't mean anything to me, and I'm not really sure why it should be important to you." Paul deals with this matter, beginning with verse 12.

The first thing the apostle does is link the resurrection of Christ to our hope of resurrection, saying that they stand or fall together. I suppose it is possible to make an intellectual distinction. You can say, "The resurrection of Jesus is one thing. My resurrection—if there ever is one—is another. There is no necessary logical connection between them." But Paul cuts through that sophistry. He argues that if there is a resurrection in one case, there can certainly be a resurrection in the other. And the big question is therefore simply: Are there resurrections? If there are, then our resurrection and the resurrection of Jesus belong together, and we can cut the quibbling.

In Paul's day people were teaching that there were no resurrections. This view probably emerged from Greek philosophy which made a big distinction between spirit and flesh, insisting that salvation was in the realm of spirit, not in the realm of flesh. According to the Greeks, the way one is saved is by reason. Death is release. Paul answers this outlook as follows: "Look, if you're arguing that resurrections don't happen, then the resurrection of Jesus did not happen. If the dead are not raised, Jesus is not raised. Think it through. Then see that if Jesus has not been raised, your faith is futile and you are still in your sins. The gospel is useless so far as any spiritual gain is concerned" (cf. vv. 16-17).

"Moreover," Paul says, "our preaching is also useless and we are discovered to be false witnesses" (cf. vv. 14-15). It must have taken a great deal of courage to say that, but I can wish that all preachers had the same courage. There are many who do not believe in the resurrection. Polls taken among today's ministers show that high percentages do not believe in the resurrection. Some time ago a poll showed that among ministers without a seminary education about 40 percent did not believe that Jesus was raised from the dead bodily. Among those who had some seminary education, the figure was higher, around 60 percent. Seminary graduates were in the 70-percent range. But if, God forbid, one had gone on to take a doctoral degree, the percentage of unbelief was in the 80s. Eighty percent did not believe in Christ's resurrection! I wish men who have come to that conclusion, whether honestly or not, would have the same kind of logical consistency possessed by Paul—that is, if there is no resurrection, then their preaching is useless—and stop preaching. I wish they would make more room for those who do believe it.

Faith is supposed to deal with the supernatural, the dimension of reality that goes beyond the merely physical. The resurrection is evidence of that dimension. If there is no resurrection, there is no supernatural element. Nothing has meaning but the life you now have, and you might as well do as the heathen do: "Let us eat and drink and be merry for tomorrow we die" (v. 32).

True preaching will not let you fool around with Christianity. It will force you to settle the question. Did Jesus rise from the dead? If you can answer that question in the negative honestly, if you can say, "No, he did not; the evidence does not support that conclusion," then forget about religion. Get on with life, enjoy yourself while you have the chance. But if Jesus did rise from the dead, then the same logic applies. Stop fooling around with Christianity. Make your commitment to Christ and get on with the serious business of living for God. This life is not the end. There is a life beyond.

One day you will stand before your Maker, and you will answer for what you have done in this body. God forbid that you should say, "Well, yes, I kind of did believe in the resurrection. But I, you know, I lived in the world and for the world, and I took my pleasure where I could find it. I acted as if the future would take care of itself, and, well, here I am. I have nothing to offer you. I have been a bad servant."

In verse 20 Paul introduces the sweep of God's plan in history. He goes back to Adam and talks about how we have all died in Adam. He moves up to the time of Christ and shows how in Him we have life. He calls Christ the firstfruits of the resurrection. Next He moves to the full harvest, to the time of the resurrection of all believers. Finally, lest we have missed what He is doing, He brings us to the kingdom of God, saying, "Then the end will come, when he [Christ] hands over the kingdom to God the Father after he has destroyed all dominion, authority and power. . . . When he has done this, then the Son himself will be made subject to him who put everything under him, so that God may be all in all" (vv. 24, 28).

Learn to think in terms of God's revealed plan for history. See that in this plan the resurrection is not incidental. It is not something that Christians like to get hold of from time to time to encourage themselves, as if they were saying, "Wouldn't it be nice if . . ?" That is not the case at all. If the resurrection is true, then in one sense it is the most important fact of all, because it shows how you fit into the great sweep of God's plan—all the way from the Fall of Adam to the life, death, and resurrection of Christ, and then on to your own resurrection and the establishment of the kingdom of God forever. You are to be part of that and to take your place with God's people.

WHAT KIND OF BODY?

In his next section Paul deals with questions. Someone might say at this point, "I understand what you are teaching, and it is all very glorious. I believe it. I am glad to be a part of it. But I do have questions, and one of them is: After all, we do all die, and we don't see many resurrections, only the resurrection of Jesus. When we think carefully, as you have encouraged us to do, we have to wonder: How are the dead raised? How is that going to work out? With what kind of body will they come?" (cf. v. 35).

Paul replies that having questions along this line shows foolishness where spiritual things are concerned. The older versions say, "Thou fool," but Paul did not mean that quite the way it sounds. He meant merely that this is foolish thinking. Why? Because we should know that the principle of being buried and raised to new life is something God has demonstrated in nature for our edification. It is the natural thing to expect, even if we do not fully understand it. When you plant a grain of wheat or corn, it seems to die. It disappears from sight. But after awhile something quite new and different is produced. The resurrection is like that: death, but new life; change, but also continuity. Paul says that this should give us a certain natural expectation of the resurrection.

"Yes, but I still don't understand it. After all, that little grain produces other grain just like it. Wheat produces wheat. Corn produces corn. Are our resurrection bodies going to be exactly like the bodies we have now? Is that what is going to happen?"

Paul makes a distinction at this point, saying, "Understand that when we are raised from death we are not going to be raised to this present kind of life but to a new, heavenly life. Therefore, just as there is a body that is appropriate to an earthly, physical existence, so is there a body that is appropriate to a spiritual, heavenly existence." If we could ask Paul to explain that, I think he might say, "I am not sure I can, at least not fully. I do not have my resurrection body yet. I do not know precisely what it will be like." But I think he might also note that we have some clues perhaps from the resurrection body of Jesus Christ. It passed through closed doors. It seemed to be able to come and go at will. Yet it was a real body. He said, "Touch me . . . a ghost does not have flesh and bones, as you see I have" (Luke 24:39).

All we really need to understand is that there is a heavenly body and an earthly body, and the earthly body cannot enter heaven, any more than corruption can inherit incorruption. God will give us the kind of body that is suitable for life in His presence.

VICTORY THROUGH CHRIST

That leads to Paul's final point. When he talks about the new body we are going to receive, he begins to think of our bodies' transformation, and it occurs to him that transformation is to be seen not merely in the resurrection of those whose bodies have died, but also in those who will still be living when the Lord comes. Paul calls this a "mystery" because it was not known beforehand. One can imagine his saying, "But now it is known: Jesus is going to return, and when He returns He is going to usher in the consummation of all things. Some will be dead; their bodies will be transformed and raised to meet the Lord in the air. Some will be living; their bodies will be changed, apart from death, so that their status will be exactly the same as those who have died. When that happens death will be swallowed up in victory, and sin will be defeated."

Paul is not thinking of the kind of victory over death that we talk about when we talk only of Jesus' resurrection. We say that because Jesus was raised from the dead, death was therefore defeated where He was concerned. He will not die again. That is true, but that is not what Paul is saying. He is saying, "True and glorious as that may be, when we talk about the saints being transformed at the final resurrection, there is an even greater truth, because at that time death will be abolished forever. It will no longer exist." It is of that day that Paul says, "Where, O death, is your victory? Where, O death, is your sting? The sting of death is sin, and the power of sin is the law. But thanks be to God! He gives us the victory through our Lord Jesus Christ" (vv. 55-57).

The conclusion is this: "Therefore, my dear brothers, stand firm. Let nothing move you. Always give yourselves fully to the work of the Lord, because you know that your labor in the Lord is not in vain" (v. 58).

If there is no resurrection, our labor in the Lord *is* in vain. There is no point to it. There is no point in serving a dead Lord, and there is no point in serving other people. But if there is a resurrection, then it makes sense to do what Paul concludes.

Stand firm; you stand upon the rock of God's truth. Let nothing move you; there are things that will try. Give yourself fully to the work of the Lord; your labor is not in vain. So long as I know that—that my labor in the Lord is not in vain—then I will keep at it no matter what the difficulty, no matter what the persecution, no matter what the ridicule. I am going to keep at it no matter what the obstacles may be. The victory does not lie with the world; it lies with Jesus and the kingdom of God.

13. *Death Vanquished*

I do not need to say a great deal about the importance of 1 Corinthians 15 so far as the resurrection is concerned. Next to the resurrection accounts in the gospels, the chapter is of the greatest importance. What I have discovered to be quite interesting, however, is that it deals with what we consider a depressing subject as much or even more than it deals with the glorious theme of the resurrection. I am talking about death. The two are connected because it is only as we come to appreciate the significance and horror of death that we understand the importance and glory of the resurrection.

In 1 Corinthians 15 the words *death, die,* or *died* occur twenty-five times, and there are other words used to say nearly the same thing: perishable, mortality, sleep. By contrast the word *resurrection,* or *raised,* occurs only twenty-four times, though there are also other words or phrases that suggest it.

Paul is writing about the resurrection to answer questions that were raised about it in the church at Corinth, but he finds himself unable to do so without talking about death, for which resurrection is the answer. Death is a very serious subject. But the joy of this passage is that death is conquered: "Where, O death, is your victory? Where, O death, is your sting? . . . But thanks be to God! He gives us the victory through our Lord Jesus Christ" (vv. 55, 57).

Death an Enemy

The first affirmation is that death is an enemy. That is said early in the chapter in clear language: "The last enemy to be destroyed is death" (v. 26).

It is important to stress this because some forms of Christianity encourage a false optimism that denies the great evils—sin, suffering, and death. There is a perversion of Christianity that carries this outlook to an extreme: Christian Science (which is not Christianity at all though it uses the name *Christian*). But the tendency is often present in true Christian circles too. We sometimes see it in relation to a person who is dying. Some time ago I read the story of a Christian who was in the last stages of cancer and who described what had been happening to her. She said, "I can see the people who come to visit me because there is a mirror in the hall, and they are reflected as they come by. Many pause to put on a pleasant expression. Then they come into the room and talk about what is going to be taking place at church the next week or the week after that. They speak of the time when I am going to be better and be with them again. But they know I won't be. They know I'm dying. I know I'm dying. They don't want to talk about it. So they put on a pleasant face and pretend the evil isn't there."

In the case of this person there was a triumphant faith in Jesus who rose from the dead and gives eternal life to all who believe in him—in addition to an awareness of the evil. Death in that room was transformed. But it is not always so. More often, as in the case of the friends, there is a denial of death, the final enemy.

Do we deny death because we think that somehow it is more spiritual to pretend that death is not real? I do not know. But I do know that this is not successful. Try doing that with sin. Say, "Sin is not sin." See if that is more spiritual. Pretend that homosexuality is all right, that pornographic films are not bad, that economic injustice or racial oppression do not exist. If you do that, you lose the cutting edge of Christian social concern and reform, and evil soon grows to intolerable levels. Well, if you cannot operate that way in the area of social evil, you cannot operate that way in regard to death. Because, while in one sense denial might satisfy *us* if we are not now facing death—at least to the extent that we are not thinking about it—it hardly satisfies anybody who is face to face with that reality. A false optimism does no good.

Moreover, we have the example of the Lord Jesus Christ, who wept at the tomb of Lazarus (John 11:35). Why did He weep? Some have reacted against the thought that Jesus could weep in the face of death. They have said, "He was going to raise Lazarus from the dead. Why should He weep? He must have been weeping about the unbelief that was around Him." Well, there was unbelief. But there was unbelief around Him at other times also, and He did not weep then. Here He was identifying with the tragedy of the situation. He was identifying with Mary and Martha in their grief. He recognized that death is an enemy. So must we. We must begin by facing that.

THE ULTIMATE ENEMY

We need to add something else. Death is not only an enemy; it is the *ultimate* enemy, the greatest enemy there is. I think we sense this in our fear of death. All are afraid of death, even Christians, though death is transformed for them, and fear is often conquered. Why is death frightening? The reason is that death means separation. We talk about death as departure. We talk about expiring; that means the departure of the spirit. Physical death is the separation of the soul and spirit from the body.

But there is another reason for fear. Death is also encounter—encounter with God. Even in the unsaved person there is the awareness that this is so. If death were just the end and if it were simply a matter of lying down and expiring, the death of a man or woman would be no more tragic than the death of an animal. But men and women sense that there is more than this. They sense that there is a life beyond death and that there is a God to be reckoned with. They know, deep in their hearts, that they have offended this God. They have sinned against Him and have failed to come to terms with Him. It is the anticipation of an encounter with God and a reckoning with Him that makes death such a terror for the unsaved. Unfortunately, even Christians are not always so sure of their relationship with God as they could be and are therefore also fearful.

AN ULTIMATE VICTORY

But we have to say—it is at this point that we begin to experience the joy—that while Paul speaks of death as the ultimate enemy, he at the same time also speaks of an ultimate victory. It is provided for by the Lord Jesus Christ. Paul speaks about it in terms of our own resurrection: "When the perishable has been clothed with the imperishable, and the mortal with immortality, then the saying that is written will come true: 'Death has been swallowed up in victory'" (v. 54). He concludes with an expression of praise: "But thanks be to God! He gives us the victory through our Lord Jesus Christ" (v. 57). What a victory that is! What a victory to know that death for the Christian is not a final separation! It is an entrance of the soul and spirit into the presence of God, to be followed in God's own time by a physical resurrection.

Death involves every part of our being. When God said to Adam and Eve in the garden, "You must not eat from the tree of the knowledge of good and evil, for when you eat of it you will surely die" (Genesis 2:17), they ate of it and died. They died in every part of their being. They had a spirit, soul, and body, and they died in each one. They died in spirit and showed it by hiding from God. They died in soul, for all the anger, lust, hate, jealousy, pride, and other sins we know began to enter the experience of the race. Finally, their bodies died also.

When God saves us He saves us in spirit, soul, and body. He gives us a new spirit in the moment of the new birth. He creates a new soul through the process of sanctification. At the resurrection He gives us a new body. So it becomes not just a spiritual salvation, not just a soul salvation, but a *whole* salvation. God made us spirit, soul, and body, and He intends us to be spirit, soul, and body.

We have a description of this final victory in 1 Thessalonians, where Paul is again answering questions that arose in the churches. The Gentiles did not have much of a background in this area. Their understanding of the afterlife was based upon Platonic philosophy in which only the soul and spirit were of value. The body was linked to earth; it drags us down. According to Platonism, salvation is to be free of the body. This was their background. So when Paul came preaching from an entirely different perspective their questions lingered, and they asked about these matters again and again.

At Thessalonica the particular questions concerned the doctrine of the Lord's return. So Paul wrote to answer their questions and explain how the Lord's return affects us. "Brothers, we do not want you to be ignorant about those who fall asleep, or to grieve like the rest of men, who have no hope. We believe that Jesus died and rose again and so we believe that God will bring with Jesus those who have fallen asleep in him" (1 Thessalonians 4:13-14). In other words, when Jesus descends to this earth, they are going to descend as well. There is a downward motion. But then there is another motion. The downward motion is the descent of the soul and spirit of those who are with the Lord Jesus Christ, but there is also an ascension, a raising of the bodies of those who have died and, therefore, obviously a reuniting of the two in God's presence.

Here is how Paul says it: "According to the Lord's own word, we tell you that we who are still alive, who are left till the coming of the Lord, will certainly not precede those who have fallen asleep. For the Lord himself will come down from heaven [the direction], with a loud command, with the voice of the archangel and with the trumpet call of God, and the dead in Christ [their bodies] will rise first." Then he goes on to explain the matter from the perspective of those who are alive at Christ's coming. "After that, we who are still alive and are left will be caught up with them in the clouds to meet the Lord in the air. And so we will be with the Lord forever" (vv. 15-18).

That is a great consummation. It is that to which Paul is looking at the end of the chapter.

A PRESENT VICTORY

Fourth, not only is death an enemy, not only is it the ultimate enemy, and not only is there an ultimate victory over death for us through the work of Christ, there is also a present victory now. The resurrection of the Lord has transformed even the kind of death that we know now.

I believe that before the coming of the Lord Jesus Christ believers who died went to what the Lord described (in speaking to the thief on the cross) as Paradise. In His story about the rich man and Lazarus He called it "Abraham's bosom." It was a place of happiness, but it was not heaven. In the Old Testament the abode of the dead is called Sheol, or Hades. It had two parts. It had a part known as Abraham's bosom or Paradise, where those who died in faith went awaiting the resurrection, and it had a place of torment where Christ placed the rich man in His parable. Neither of these was in the presence of God Himself. Thus, when the Lord promised the thief on the cross that He would be with him that day, the day on which they both died, He did not say, "Today you will be with me in the presence of my Father in heaven." He said, "Today you will be with me in paradise" (Luke 23:43). When the Lord died He went to Paradise and there proclaimed the benefits of His death to those who had died in anticipation of it. When He arose he carried these into heaven for the first time, leading "captives in his train" and giving "gifts to men," as Ephesians 3:8 says. This was the time at which the tombs were opened and the dead who had died in faith went into the city of Jerusalem and revealed themselves to living believers.

The point I am making is that death was transformed by Christ's work. Before, there was at best only a vague hope in the afterlife. It was the hope of the Old Testament saints. Job, David, and the others expected God to be faithful to them even though worms should destroy their bodies. They had faith, but it was not very well informed or articulated. Now things are different—because of the resurrection of Jesus—and Paul can write as he does in his letter to the Corinthians, saying that he "would prefer to be away from the body and at home with the Lord" (2 Corinthians 5:8). He can say, in writing to the Philippians, that though he has a desire to remain with them for their good, nevertheless death is "better by far" because it means entrance into the presence of God forever (Philippians 1:23). That is what death is for us. It is entrance into God's presence.

This We Know

Finally, I want you to see that we have assurance of these things because of Christ's resurrection. Apart from that, these ideas would be mere philosophy, perhaps mysticism. They might be true, but they would not have the cutting edge, the force of conviction and assurance that they actually do have for Christian people. Where does our conviction originate? It comes only from the factual certainty of Christ's own death and resurrection.

Christ's was a real death. Unless it was a real death we are not talking about a real resurrection. Jesus really died. Unbelievers who for some reason cannot avoid writing about Christianity usually try to deny one of the two. They either deny that there was a real resurrection or they deny that there was a real death. There have been elaborate theories worked out to deny the death; this was particularly so in the nineteenth century. Some suggested that the Lord only swooned and then revived in the tomb, or that the authorities crucified the wrong person. Theories like those were seriously developed. But today not even the most liberal scholars would take this line. Jesus really died. If anything is a fact in history, it is this: the death of Jesus Christ under Pontius Pilate.

At the same time it is not just a real death that confronts us. It is also a real resurrection: a real resurrection with a real body and a real person standing there who could be handled and touched, the kind of person who could eat broiled fish to demonstrate that reality. He was no ghost.

I wonder if you have noticed that when Hollywood tries to portray these things in movies it inevitably spiritualizes the resurrection. I once saw that sort of film on television. There was the death. It was real enough. When the Roman soldier took his hammer and drove the nail through the hand, there was no doubt that it was real metal and flesh and wood. The death was real. But then the resurrection came, and all you could hear was music. You could not even see the Lord. People rushed about in the joy of the resurrection. But where was Jesus? I looked for Him. At last there was a ghostly view of Him floating off into the clouds. This was no resurrection! If the resurrection had been like that I guarantee that Thomas for one would not have believed in it, and I do not think that Peter and John would have either. The resurrection was not like that; it was a real flesh-and-blood resurrection, and these men knew it when they touched Christ's body. Because of this they were willing to go out from an obscure corner to every corner of the Roman Empire proclaiming the Lord's death and resurrection. They were willing to be crucified themselves rather than deny their Lord. That is how real it was. A mythical resurrection does not give this kind of conviction, but a real resurrection does.

ON CHRIST THE ROCK

Paul's conclusion is in verse 58. He tells us to stand firm, be unmovable, and give ourselves fully to the Lord's work. Notice that he does not say we are going to be successful in the Lord's work—though we hope we may be. He does not say that we are going to be accepted by others for doing the Lord's work—though we hope there will be a degree of acceptance also. He does say that we are to stand firm and be steadfast in it, and that we cannot do so unless we believe in the resurrection.

Do we believe in it? Will we do Christ's work? Will we be unmovable?

There is work to be done. If we take the message of Easter and merely go out with a mystical gleam in our eye and say, "Oh, isn't it wonderful that Jesus rose from the dead?" and let that be the end of it, we are not much better than the liberal theologians. But if we say, "Jesus rose with a real body in a real world and in a real way and with a real voice commissioned His disciples to do real work, until they in His own time die and are raised again also in real bodies to be with Him," then we have grasped the point and can live differently.

You say in the midst of a world like ours, threatened as it is by suffering, death, hostility, sin—all these things—"But how can I stand firm?" The answer is that you can stand firm if you stand upon Jesus. We sing it in one of our hymns:

> His oath, his covenant, his blood,
> Support me in the whelming flood;
> When all around my soul gives way,
> He then is all my hope and stay.
>
> On Christ, the solid Rock, I stand;
> All other ground is sinking sand.

All other ground *is* sinking sand. But Jesus is the Rock. He is the rock the builders rejected but which has now become our foundation and the foundation of God's church.

14. *Remember the Resurrection*

T here are many facts in life that we are called upon to remember—appointments, vital pieces of information, names of acquaintances, even incidents from the past that are supposed to have significance. "Remember the Alamo" was a rallying cry to Texans at the time of the war with Mexico. "Remember the Maine" served the same purpose at the time of the Spanish American War, following the sinking of the USS *Maine* in Havana harbor in 1898. In World War II the saying was "Remember Pearl Harbor." The interesting fact about these sayings is that each refers to a defeat. The saying that I want to discuss now is different. It is the remembrance of a victory.

The challenge comes from a letter of the aged apostle Paul to his son in the faith, the young preacher Timothy. Paul had been courageous and energetic in carrying the gospel to the civilized world of his day. He had preached in Syria and Cilicia, Cyprus, Asia Minor, Macedonia, Greece, and Italy. Now he was in prison and was writing a letter of advice and encouragement to the man who was to carry on much of his work.

He says in effect, "Timothy, do you want your preaching to be strong and effective, as my preaching was? Do you want to win souls? Do you want to see the church remain strong? Well, then, do not forget the great foundational truths of Christianity. And, in particular, do not forget the resurrection." His exact words are "Remember Jesus Christ, raised from the dead, descended from David" (2 Timothy 2:8). In that statement we have an effective clue to the success of Paul's ministry as well as an indication of how we can be effective in our own. Remember the resurrection! We can forget many things about life, even many things about Christianity. But if we remember the resurrection, we will always have a gospel that has power to change men's souls.

A SIMPLE GOSPEL

We need to ask some questions about Paul's statement. Paul writes, "Remember Jesus Christ, raised from the dead." But we might argue, "Paul, we know what you are saying, but why is that so important? Why do you stress the resurrection?"

There are a number of answers. First, we should remember the resurrection because as long as we remember it we will always have a *simple* gospel, and a simple gospel is what men need.

Understand, I am not talking about a "simplistic" gospel. A simplistic gospel would be one that is superficial, that does not really appreciate the problems or properly grapple with the facts. No one wants simplistic answers in any area of life, certainly not in Christianity. But I am not talking about a simplistic gospel. I am talking about a "simple" gospel, and a simple gospel is something else. It is a gospel that is simple because it brings simplicity to areas that would be hopelessly confused without it. Probably all great scientific and intellectual breakthroughs are simple in this sense. Before them there was confusion. Afterward there was clarity and light. It is that way with the Christian gospel, centered in the life, death, and resurrection of Jesus Christ. The resurrection is the capstone of Christianity. Accept that and the rest falls into place. Believe in the resurrection, and you have no difficulty with the other miracles, the full divinity of Jesus, the inspiration of the Scriptures, and a host of other things. Together these truths simplify man's need and speak of that simple (though profound) remedy which God has provided in Christ.

It is a pity that Christian preaching does not always sound a clear note on this theme. Instead of the clear and certain sound of the trumpet, we often hear musical variations, and the truth is lost. When the noted Swiss theologian Karl Barth was in this country a number of years before his death, he was invited to speak to the National Press Club in Washington. Carl F. Henry, founding editor of *Christianity Today*, presented him to the other reporters and then said: "Dr. Barth, you have written a good deal about the resurrection of Jesus Christ, and you are standing before men who are accustomed to reporting unusual events. Tell us, according to your outlook, if these men had been present in the garden on that first Easter morning, would they have seen anything that they could later have reported in their papers?"

Barth proceeded to give a complex answer, which, as anyone who knows his theology would imagine, had to do with the belief that miracles are not actually a part of history but rather are tangential to it. They are real, according to Barth, but unobservable.

When Barth finished, Carl Henry turned and asked a reporter who was near him, "Did you understand what he said?"

"I'm not sure," the reporter answered, "but I think I did. I think he said 'No.'"

People do not need that kind of confusion, and the true nature of the resurrection does not encourage it. Christ rose, literally and bodily. We believe that. We teach it. Moreover, people understand such teaching. Once, when the late President Harry Truman and his fellow democrat Adlai Stevenson were together on the upper floor of a modern office building, Stevenson was bemoaning his traditional lack of success in politics.

"What am I doing wrong, Harry?" he is said to have asked.

Truman walked to the window and pointed to the milling people many floors below. "You don't speak to the man down there," he replied.

Unfortunately, Christians often fail to do that too. But we need not fail, so long as we have a gospel that is based on an historical and demonstrable resurrection.

A Supernatural Gospel

Second, we should remember the resurrection because so long as we remember it we will always have a *supernatural* gospel.

Are you not just a bit tired of schemes for human betterment, particularly since they do not really seem to be solving deep human problems or improving our environment? You do not even have to be a Christian to be disenchanted.

Some years ago a leading news magazine published a special series of essays under the general title "Second Thoughts About Man." It was a good series, designed to examine the areas of modern life that have most often been looked to for solutions to the problems of crime, poverty, prejudice, and others that trouble us. The conclusion, which was intended to reflect the views of those in the fields of behavioral psychology, religion, education, and science, was simply that those lines of approach have failed and that probably all purely human attempts to deal with man's perverse nature will also prove fruitless.

The magazine said, "At the heart of the ferment of the '70s is a deep, even humble perception that man and his universe are more complex than he recently thought. . . . Optimism has bred a false enthusiasm that this method or that system was somehow the answer. Now some of the growing skepticism questions whether any system can ever fully surmount the recalcitrance and perversity of man."[1]

If the behavioral psychologists, religious figures, educators, and scientists are telling us that the ultimate hope for man is not to be found in the fields in which they are working, where is that hope to be found? They are not saying that there is no good in what they are doing. They are accomplishing much and are rightly proud of it. But they are saying that the best they can do has limits and that the ultimate problems lie deep in man's nature and are beyond mere human control. They cannot solve them. What can? The answer is: something beyond man and nature, something superhuman and supernatural.

1. *Time*, 2 April 1973, p. 78.

That is what Christianity offers. It requires us to remember the resurrection. The resurrection is proof of new life and great power. It was seen in Christ; it can be seen in anybody who will commit himself to Christ through faith and thus be united to Him by the Spirit of God. Christ can change lives. He *has* changed lives. He has done in millions that which no power of earth could ever accomplish. I am glad to recommend a gospel that is frankly supernatural and that can therefore change both ourselves and our society.

A SCRIPTURAL GOSPEL

Third, we are to remember the resurrection because so long as we remember it we will always have a *scriptural* gospel. Our faith will not be a novelty. Instead, we will have a faith linked—as all true faith must be linked—to God's great purposes in human history.

That truth was important to the early preachers of the gospel, for they were proud of the antiquity of the faith and commended it to their contemporaries partially on that ground. Jesus taught that all that happened to Him happened because it was foretold in the Scriptures. After His resurrection, for instance, we read that Jesus "opened their minds so they could understand the Scriptures. He told them, 'This is what is written: The Christ will suffer and rise from the dead on the third day'" (Luke 24:45-46). Paul later wrote that he delivered to the Corinthians that gospel which he had first received, "that Christ died for our sins according to the Scriptures, that he was buried, that he was raised on the third day according to the Scriptures" (1 Corinthians 15:3, 4).

Peter preached that David had written of Christ's resurrection: "You will not abandon me to the grave, nor will you let your Holy One see decay" (Acts 2:27; see Psalm 16:10). Others of the early preachers did likewise. Those men were conscious of the fact that what they were called to proclaim was eternal. It was no novelty. It was the overriding theme of the universe. It was that which had been proclaimed from before the beginning of the world and would be proclaimed to the end.

We preach no novelty, no fads. America is filled with fads. Americans are idealistic, but they have a hard time deciding what the source of their idealism will be. Every year the crusade changes. Yesterdays' burning issue is forgotten and another takes its place. Our faith is not like that. It is not so ephemeral. Our gospel is not something man dreamed up in the twentieth century. It is God's eternal plan, known in all ages by people who have known Him. We are part of that company. We are one with Abraham, Isaac, and Jacob; with David the king, Isaiah the prophet, and all the other prophets; with James and Peter and John, with the early church Fathers, the later church Fathers, the Reformers—Luther, Calvin, Zwingli, and others—and with those from our own time also.

We will remember that if we remember Christ's resurrection.

A Satisfying Gospel

Finally, we are to remember the resurrection of Jesus Christ because, if we do remember it, we will always have a *satisfying* gospel. The truth of the resurrection of Jesus Christ satisfies.

There is much in life that is not satisfying. We may be satisfied for a time. But the pleasures soon pale and satisfaction fades. When we are young and life lies before us, the offerings of the world are not bad, it seems. There is an appeal to fame or wealth or companionship. The hunger of the imagination paints our goals in bright colors. We live on dreams. But what happens when the future doesn't bring what we ask for? What happens in the face of suffering, death, or sorrow? What happens in old age? If there is nothing more to life than the things that time takes from us, life becomes misery. On the other hand, if we are united to the living Lord Jesus Christ who has gone before to prepare for us a place in His presence, then life retains its meaning and is filled with joy.

We find an illustration of this in the second chapter of 2 Timothy. Paul is writing to Timothy. But where was Paul? Paul was in prison. There had been times of great liberty when he was free to preach the gospel wherever he wished and to whoever would listen. But now he was confined. Those days were over. Soon his life would be ended. Does Paul complain? Is there bitterness? Does he regret his commitment to Christ? Not at all! He rejoices! Thus, a little farther along in the chapter we find him declaring,

Here is a trustworthy saying:

> If we died with him,
>   we will also live with him;
> if we endure,
>   we will also reign with him.
> If we disown him,
>   he will also disown us;
> if we are faithless,
>   he will remain faithful,
>   for he cannot disown himself.
>   (2 Timothy 2:11-13)

Paul found that the gospel of the crucified and resurrected Lord was satisfying even at the end of life and in suffering.

Have you remembered the resurrection of Jesus Christ? If you have, you have a gospel that is simple, supernatural, scriptural, and satisfying. You have something that you will be able to communicate to those who need it desperately.

15. *Four Words for Easter Sunday*

I have noticed that when something important happens the words with which we first learn of the event are often remembered. At the birth of our first child, we remember what the nurse or doctor said and visualize the scene. Some of us remember how we first heard of the end of World War II or the beginning of it. We remember hearing of the death of a friend, a promotion, the election of a president, the landing of the first men on the moon.

It may be as a result of this tendency that the words we are about to study—the words that first announced the resurrection of Jesus Christ from the dead—were remembered by the women who heard them, were passed on to others, and were eventually preserved for us in Matthew's gospel.

Certainly the women were in no frame of mind to have remembered those words had they not been so important. To begin with, they obviously were not expecting the resurrection, for they had come to the garden tomb to anoint the Lord's body. Besides, they had their minds on other matters. "What about the stone?" they were asking. Probably they were also worried about the guards. At last, having approached the tomb and having seen the angel, their earlier concerns with the stone gave way to fright, and they had to be reassured by the heavenly messenger: "Do not be afraid, for I know that you are looking for Jesus, who was crucified. He is not here; he has risen, just as he said" (Matthew 28:5-6).

I can imagine that the senses and memory of those women were sharpened to an extraordinary pitch as they heard the angel continue: "Come and see the place where he lay. Then go quickly and tell his disciples: 'He has risen from the dead'" (vv. 6-7). Can we also hear those words sharply today? Can we remember them? I think that we both can and should, for they contain a message for us just as certainly as they contained a message for Mary (the wife of Cleopas), Salome, and their friends.

The angel's message contains four great imperatives upon which the entire communication rests: come, see, go, and tell. We must *come* to the tomb, *see* the place where the Lord lay, and then *go* and *tell* others about his resurrection.

AN INVITATION TO COME

The first word is *come*. That is important, for there is much to hinder one from coming. We can imagine how that would have been true for the women. The place itself might have hindered them. It was a graveyard early in the morning, clearly not the most attractive place to be. The women could have failed to come for that reason. They could have said to each other, "Let's go home; we'll come back later when we have more people with us or when it's lighter."

The edict of Rome might have hindered them. The tomb had been sealed by Pilate's orders. Soldiers were stationed to guard it. But something unusual had happened; the stone had been removed. That meant the seal had been broken. Rome had been disobeyed. The women might have said, "We cannot go closer. Rome forbids it. We cannot look in."

Or again, their own sin might have hindered their coming. Here was something holy, something miraculous. They might have said, "We are unclean; we cannot come." If they had said any of those things, we would have understood them. For we recognize that fear, secular authority, and sin often keep one from the Savior.

Yet the women were not hindered by those things. Here was an invitation to come forward, the same kind of invitation that the Lord Jesus Christ had given on so many occasions. The women recognized the authentic voice of God in the invitation and obeyed it.

I wonder if you have obeyed that invitation. The Lord Jesus Christ, through the Scriptures and through the preaching of the gospel, gives an invitation to all to come to Him. He has given that invitation to you. "Come to me, all you who are weary and burdened, and I will give you rest. Take my yoke upon you and learn from me, for I am gentle and humble in heart, and you will find rest for your souls" (Matthew 11:28-29). Have you come? Have you responded to that invitation? There is no growth in the Christian life, no increase in knowledge or wisdom, until you first respond to it.

So the first word is a very practical one, the word *come*.

A FURTHER INVITATION

Second, the angel said, "*See* the place where the Lord lay." That is a further and quite interesting invitation, I think. For when we ask, "Why should we see the place where the Lord lay?" the answers are instructive. Think for a minute about why we should see the grave and how we may profit by it.

First, we see the grave that we might understand *the condescension of the Lord Jesus Christ*. The Lord Jesus Christ is not just a man for whom such a death would be natural. Jesus is the Lord! Jehovah! The Savior! Christ! Messiah! He is the one who dwelt with God in all eternity—who was God, equal to God, equal in all power and glory—yet laid aside the glory to take upon Himself the form of a man in order that He might die to save us. Oh, the condescension of such a God who would come from the glories of heaven to this earth and then die and lie in such a tomb! When we look at the grave we see there the love and condescension of our Lord.

We see something else too. We see *the horror of our sin*, for our sin placed Him there. He did not die for His own sin; He was sinless. He died in our place. "He was pierced for our transgressions, he was crushed for our iniquities; the punishment that brought us peace was upon him, and by his wounds we are healed" (Isaiah 53:5). When we see the place where the Lord lay and say, "It is my sin that brought Him to that end," we begin to develop a proper awareness of sin and hatred for it.

The third reason we should see the tomb is that we might be reminded of *where we also will lie*. Unless the Lord comes for His own before that moment, we too must die. There is a time when we will be separated from all that we now know. We will leave friends and loved ones behind. We will leave our material possessions. We look to the tomb and learn of our mortality. It teaches us that there is a life beyond this life for which we must prepare.

Fourth and most important, we look at the tomb not just to see the love and condescension of our Lord, not just to see the horror of our sin, not just to be reminded that we too must die, but we look to the tomb to see that *Jesus is not in it now.* He is risen! He has conquered death! That is the one great evidence for the resurrection.

Most of those who have written in a serious and analytical way about the events of those early weeks notice—if they are honest—that in all the reports we have, whether in the New Testament or those preserved indirectly by secular writers such as Josephus or in the Jewish Talmud, there is not one instance of any attempt to deny that the grave was empty.

Sometimes there is the argument—which is also reported in our New Testament—that the disciples came and stole the body. But not one writer, either secular or religious, denies that the tomb was empty and the body gone. What accounts for it? Not theft by the enemies of Christ; for if they had had the body they would have produced it later when claims of a resurrection were made by the disciples. Not theft by the disciples either; for if they had stolen the body, they would not have been willing to die (as many of them did later) for what they knew to be a fabrication. The tomb was empty because Christ had risen.

While we are looking at the tomb we notice a fifth lesson. It is not only that Jesus rose from the dead, but that *we shall rise also* if we are united to Him. Jesus did not come to this earth to teach, die, and rise again in order that in the end He might lose those for whom He died. He came, as the Scriptures say, "to save completely" (Hebrews 7:25) those who believe on Him. We are saved, not just in spirit in order to have fellowship with God; not just in soul in order to be transformed during the days of our earthly life, but in body also. The salvation

Jesus brings is complete. So we look to the empty tomb to see that one day we too shall rise and shall be with Him.

Charles Haddon Spurgeon, who makes some of these points in a brief way in one of his sermons, expresses his thought as follows:

> "Come, see the place where the Lord lay," to see that thou canst not lie there long. It is not the place where Jesus *is*. He is gone, and thou art to be with him where he is. Come and look at this tomb. There is no door in it. There *was* one; it was a huge rock, a monstrous stone, and none could move it. It was sealed. Seest thou not how they have set the stamp of the Sanhedrin, the stamp of the law, upon the seal, to make it sure, that none should move it? But now, if thou wilt go to the place where Jesus lay, the seal is broken, the guards are fled, the stone is gone. Such will thy tomb be.[1]

WORK TO DO

We have looked at two of the words central to the angel's message: the invitation to come and the imperative see. We have seen some of what that implies. The next word is *go*. This is a reminder that, blessed as it may be to stay near the tomb and learn its lessons, nevertheless there is work to do and we must not linger by the tomb and fail to do it.

There are some who linger. It is hard to know why. One reason may be that they are not really convinced of the resurrection. Somehow the resurrection is an embarrassment to them, and they do not want to talk too much about it. Such people cannot quite get Jesus out of their minds. So, in order to do him a favor, they focus on his death. Have you not read "lives of Jesus" that in a magnificent way build up to the atonement but then say somewhat apologetically at the end that "it was reported by certain people that he rose again on Sunday morning"? Such writers are not really sure that Jesus rose from the dead. That may be one reason why they focus on Calvary.

Another reason may be a form of false piety. In that approach Christians look to the death of Christ and are touched by it. Then, quite naturally but nevertheless wrongly, they try to work up a proper response to Christ's death by mourning over the crucifixion. Christ rose. They know it. But somehow they think that it is dishonoring to Christ to rejoice at His resurrection.

May I suggest a third reason? I think liturgical interests encourage that approach in certain branches of the Christian church. Lent is forty days long, after all, and it builds up to Good Friday. So there are forty days to sing the mournful songs about Christ being forsaken by God and stricken. Then Easter Sunday comes, and in one morning the celebration of the resurrection is over and everybody goes back to feeling sorry again.

Why do we worship on Sunday? We worship on Sunday because Sunday is the day of resurrection. Every Sunday is Easter Sunday for the Christian. So the

---

1. Charles Haddon Spurgeon, "A Visit to the Tomb" in *Metropolitan Tabernacle Pulpit*, vol. 18 (Pasadena, Tex.: Pilgrim Publications, 1971), p. 647.

emphasis should be exactly the reverse. On Good Friday, if we wish, we may set aside one day to remember Christ's death particularly. But throughout the year, Sunday after Sunday, we should remember the Lord's resurrection triumph. There are many factors that could persuade us to keep the tomb sealed and thus keep our attention focused on the body that is supposed to be there. There is the edict of Rome. There are the stone, the seal, the soldiers. But when the resurrection comes the stone is rolled away. The seal is broken. The soldiers are scattered.

For us there is the proclamation of the angel: "He is not here; he has risen, just as he said. Come and see the place where he lay. Then go quickly and tell his disciples: 'He has risen from the dead.'"

A Word to Be Spoken

That leads me to the word *tell*. It is last in the sequence—and rightly so. For if we have come, if we have seen that the tomb is empty, and if we are commissioned to go, then it is inevitable that we will have a message to tell to those we encounter. Good news must be told! If we do not tell it, we do not really recognize it for what it is.

Let me give a simple illustration that you will immediately recognize if you have ever had children hunt for Easter eggs in your home. Have you noticed that children never find an egg without telling you about it? In my home there have been three children. So the discovery of each egg was reported three times. There were twenty eggs one Easter, so there were sixty announcements. The little one would find an egg and cry, "Look, I found an egg!" Then the oldest child would confirm it. "She's right, Daddy; Jennifer found an egg!" Then the middle one would add, "Jennifer really found an egg!" One egg. Three tellings. So on for twenty eggs.

Well, the greatest news in the world is the resurrection of Jesus Christ. How, then, can we who are Christians fail to tell the world about it? You ask, "What shall we tell?" Let me suggest three things: first, that He is risen; second, that death is conquered; third, that God has made this same Jesus whom men crucified and killed both Lord and Christ. The empty tomb is the evidence. The resurrection is the proof. Do we understand that message? Then we must tell other people.

In one sense, the message of the angel is a sermon. It is a perfect sermon. I do not know how such a great sermon can be condensed into three verses, but it is. And it does not suffer from the contraction. First, there is the announcement: "He is not here; he has risen." Then there are the four imperatives, "Come," "See," "Go," "Tell"—those are the points. Finally, at the very end there is the promise: "He is going ahead of you into Galilee. There you will see him." Why is the promise important? It is important because we might be shy about the message. We might be timorous. We might be overcome with what could seem to be difficulties in making a supernatural message known to a secular world. Here were women—and women were not highly regarded in antiquity—about to go to others with the greatest message the world has ever heard. They had news so stupendous, so utterly unbelievable, that even the disciples would not believe it when they heard it. If the women had said to themselves, "But no one will believe us," they certainly would have been right, humanly speaking. Yet what does the angel say? The angel says, "He [Jesus, the risen Lord] is going ahead of you." They may have been shy, but Jesus was going ahead to mark and prepare the way.

Is the promise just for the women? No, it is for us too. Thus, just a little later on in the same chapter, when Jesus talks to the disciples and commissions them to the task of world evangelization, we find the same message. Jesus begins with His authority: "All authority in heaven and on earth has been given to me." He issues commands: "Go and *make disciples* of all nations, *baptizing* them in the name of the Father and of the Son and of the Holy Spirit, and *teaching* them to obey everything I have commanded you." And then what? "And surely I will be with you always, to the very end of the age." Those are the last words in Matthew's gospel, and they are a promise. Jesus is with us. Jesus goes before us as we go. How, then, can we fail to proclaim such a great message to the world?

16. Charge of the Risen Christ

I am sure you have noticed in your study of the Word of God that nearly all the resurrection appearances of Christ end with His telling those to whom He appeared to announce the good news. It was the case with Mary Magdelene: "Go . . . to my brothers and tell them, 'I am returning to my Father and your Father, to my God and your God'" (John 20:17). It was the case with the women who were returning from the tomb. At the tomb the angel had told them: "He is not here; he has risen, just as he said. Come and see the place where he lay. Then go quickly and tell his disciples: 'He has risen from the dead'" (Matthew 28:6-7). When Jesus appeared to them shortly thereafter He said, "Do not be afraid. Go and tell my brothers to go to Galilee; there they will see me" (v. 10). It is true with nearly all the other appearances also, particularly those more formal appearances to the disciples in which they were explicitly commissioned to the task of world evangelism.

So far as the New Testament indicates, there were at least ten appearances of the risen Lord, plus another some years later to the apostle Paul. In eight of those there is an explicit commission, and in five the command to go into all the world and preach the gospel is given formally.

Why is that? It is a reflection of the fact that if a person really believes that Jesus of Nazareth was raised from the dead on that first Easter Sunday and understands the significance of that fact, it will be virtually impossible for him or her to keep silent about it.

Do we keep silent? In one of his books, evangelist and Bible teacher Reuben A. Torrey tells of his first meeting with D. L. Moody in the spring of 1878. At that time Moody was holding meetings in New Haven, Connecticut, and he was there on Easter Sunday. He rose early in the morning, went out into the streets and, as he met people, proclaimed this great fact to them: "Jesus is risen." So also should we go out today to proclaim this risen and reigning Christ to those who desperately need to meet Him. We need to urge them to receive Him as their own dear Savior.

As I have thought along those lines I have been impressed with the fact that Matthew ends his life of Christ on that note. He does not end it with the resurrection itself. Even more striking, he does not include an account of Christ's ascension. Instead, he ends his gospel with Christ's Great Commission. Apparently it was evident to him, as it should also be to us, that this is the practical point at which the life of Christ bears on our own speech and conduct. Matthew reports,

> Then the eleven disciples went to Galilee, to the mountain where Jesus had told them to go. When they saw him, they worshiped him; but some doubted. Then Jesus came to them and said, "All authority in heaven and on earth has been given to me. Therefore go and make disciples of all nations, baptizing them in the name of the Father and of the Son and of the Holy Spirit, and teaching them to obey everything I have commanded you. And surely I will be with you always, to the very end of the age." (Matthew 28:16-20)

There are three parts to this commission. First, an announcement: "All authority in heaven and on earth has been given to me" (v. 18). Second, a command: "Therefore go and make disciples of all nations, baptizing them in the name of the Father and of the Son and of the Holy Spirit, and teaching them to obey everything I have commanded you" (vv. 19-20). Third, a promise: "And surely I will be with you always, to the very end of the age" (v. 20). It is striking that each of these parts is related to the fact and the meaning of the resurrection.

The first part of these verses deals with Christ's authority. It is in the form of an announcement: "All authority in heaven and on earth has been given to me." Is it possible for us to overestimate the scope of Christ's authority? I think not. For the announcement is not merely that authority has been given to Him but that *all* authority has been given to Him. And then, lest we still misunderstand or minimize that authority, the text declares that it is an authority exercised both in heaven and on earth.

That all authority in heaven has been given to Jesus could mean merely that the authority He was to exercise on earth would be recognized in heaven also. If that is so, it would be a statement of Christ's full divinity, for that authority is none other than Jehovah's authority. Yet there is probably more to Christ's statement than that. For one thing, when the Bible speaks about heavenly "powers" or "authorities" it is usually speaking about spiritual or demonic powers. Again, when it speaks of Christ's victory through His death and resurrection it usually has those powers in mind.

We think of Ephesians 6:12, which says of the Christian's warfare: "For our struggle is not against flesh and blood, but against the rulers, against the authorities, against the powers of this dark world and against the spiritual forces of evil in the heavenly realms." Or again, we think of those verses early in the same letter that speak of the greatness of God's power "which he exerted in Christ when he raised him from the dead and seated him at his right hand in the heavenly realms, far above all rule and authority, power and dominion, and every title that can be given, not only in the present age but also in the one to come" (Ephesians 1:20-21).

When we put Christ's announcement into that context we sense that what the Lord is talking about is not so much an acknowledgment of His earthly authority in heaven but rather a declaration that His authority is superior to and over all other authorities whether spiritual, demonic, or otherwise. His resurrection demonstrates His authority over any power that can possibly be imagined. Consequently, we do not fear Satan or anyone else while we are engaged in His service.

Second, Jesus announces that He has authority over everything on earth. That has several dimensions. It means that He has authority over us, His people. How can it be otherwise? If we are truly His people, we have come to Him confessing that we are sinners and He is the divine Savior and that we have accepted His sacrifice on our behalf and have pledged ourselves to follow Him as Lord. That is hypocrisy if it does not contain a recognition of His authority over us in every area of our lives. To be sure, there are other legitimate authorities as well. There is the authority of parents over children, of church officers over congregations, or of the state over its citizens. But those, while valid, are still lesser authorities. Jesus is the King of kings and Lord of lords. We cannot miss the fact that it is on the basis of His supreme authority over His people, which we acknowledge if we truly are His people, that Jesus utters the Great Commission.

Again, the declaration of Christ's authority on earth also means that He has authority over those who are not yet believers. That is, His authority extends to the people of the "nations" to whom He sends us with the gospel. That means, on one hand, that the religion of our Lord is to be a world religion. No one is outside the sphere of His authority or is to be exempt from His call. On the other hand, that is also a statement of His ability to bring fruit from our efforts, for it is through the exercise of His authority that men and women actually come to believe on and follow Him.

John R. W. Stott has said of Christ's authority:

> The fundamental basis of all Christian missionary enterprise is the universal authority of Jesus Christ, "in heaven and on earth." If the authority of Jesus were circumscribed on earth, if he were but one of many religious teachers, one of many Jewish prophets, one of many divine incarnations, we would have no mandate to present him to the nations as the Lord and Savior of the world. If the authority of Jesus were limited in heaven, if he had not decisively overthrown the principalities and powers, we might

still proclaim him to the nations, but we would never be able to "turn them from darkness to light, and from the power of Satan unto God" (Acts 26:18). Only because all authority on earth belongs to Christ dare we go to all nations. And only because all authority in heaven as well is his have we any hope of success.[1]

A GREAT COMMISSION

The second part of these verses contains a command. It is the Great Commission proper, and it falls into three parts. As we *go* into the world—the word *go* is a participle in Greek, which indicates that Jesus is merely assuming that will happen—we are to *"make disciples* of all nations, *baptizing* them in the name of the Father and of the Son and of the Holy Spirit, and *teaching* them to obey everything I have commanded you." That command is for all believers, not just for a core of professional evangelists. It is to be the word of all Christian people in all ages.

This Great Commission to "teach," "baptize," and then "teach" again is something that cannot be overlooked by Christian people if Jesus really is Lord. I think in that connection of a story frequently told by R. C. Sproul, founder and president of the Ligonier Valley Study Center in Pennsylvania. At the time of the story Sproul was a student at Pittsburgh Theological Seminary, taking a course from John H. Gerstner, professor of church history. The professor had given a lecture on predestination and then, as was his custom, began to ask questions of the students. Sproul was seated on one end of a large semicircle. Gerstner began at the other end. He asked the first student "Now, sir, if predestination is true, why should we be involved in evangelism?"

The student looked back at the professor and said, "I don't know."

Gerstner went to the next student, who replied, "It beats me."

The next seminarian answered, "I am glad you raised that question; I always wondered about it myself, Dr. Gerstner."

The professor kept going on around the semicircle, knocking the students off one by one.

All the while, Sproul was sitting in the corner feeling like Plato in one of Socrates' dialogues. Socrates had raised the difficult question. He had heard from all the lesser stars. Now Plato was to give the lofty answer to the impenetrable mystery of the question. Sproul was scared to death. Finally Gerstner got to him and asked, "Well, Mr. Sproul, suppose you tell us. If predestination is true, why should we be involved in evangelism?"

Sproul says that he slid down in the seat and prefaced his answer with all kinds of

---

1. John R. W. Stott, "The Great Commission," in *One Race, One Gospel, One Task: Official Reference Volumes of the World Congress on Evangelism, Berlin 1966,* ed. Carl F. H. Henry and W. Stanley Mooneyham (Minneapolis: World Wide Publications, 1967), p. 46.

apologies, saying, "Well, Dr. Gerstner, I know this isn't what you're looking for, and I know that you must be seeking for some profound, intellectual response which I am not prepared to give. But just in passing, one small point that I think we ought to notice here is that God does command us to be involved in evangelism."

Gerstner laughed and said, "Yes, Mr. Sproul, God does command us to be involved in evangelism. And, of course, Mr. Sproul, what could be more insignificant than the fact that the Lord of glory, the Savior of your soul, the Lord omnipotent, has commanded you to be involved in evangelism?" His students got the point in a hurry, and so should we if we take the authority and teaching of the Lord Jesus Christ seriously.

Moreover, Jesus does not allow His command to remain vague, for He goes on to tell us how we should do it.

First, he tells us to make disciples of all nations. In the King James Version this command is rendered "teach all nations," but the word that is translated *teach* is not the same as the word for *teach* that comes later. The later word, *didasko*, from which we get our word *didactic*, really means "teach." However, the first word is *matheteuo*, which literally means "to make one a disciple." Thus, the *Revised Standard* and *New International Version* translate this phrase "make disciples of all nations," and the *New English Bible* says similarly, "make all nations my disciples." That means, "Make them *my* disciples"—disciples of Christ. And that means preach the gospel to them so that through the power of the Scriptures and the Holy Spirit they are converted from sin to Christ and thereafter follow Him as their Lord. In this commission, evangelism is the primary and obvious task. Without it nothing else follows.

On the other hand, without what follows, evangelism is at best one-sided and perhaps even unreal. Jesus goes on to say that as a second part of His commission those who are His must lead their converts to the point of baptism "in the name of the Father and of the Son and of the Holy Spirit." That does not mean that empty rites or ceremonies are to take the place of a total heart commitment to Christ. Far from it.

Rather, it means two things. First, that at some point commitment to Jesus as Savior and Lord must become public; for baptism, as we have suggested, is a public act. It is a declaration before other believers and the world that the person being baptized intends to follow Jesus. Second, it means that he or she is now also uniting with the church, Christ's visible body. Moreover, this is natural and necessary. If we are truly converted, we will want to join with other similarly converted people. And we must, for we do belong to them.

Finally, Jesus instructs those carrying out His commission to teach others all that He has commanded them. A lifetime of learning follows the conversion of the individual and entry into church membership. Moreover, he is to learn not just the sayings spoken by Jesus while He was here on earth but rather the whole of the Bible, which He has given to us. Proper missionary work is to go out with the gospel, win men and women to Christ, bring them into the fellowship of the church, and then see that they are taught the things that are recorded in the Scriptures.

GOD WITH US

The last part of these closing verses of Matthew contains a great promise: "And surely I will be with you always, to the very end of the age." We think back to the beginning of the gospel to that passage in which the newborn Christ is named. It reads, "'The virgin will be with child and will give birth to a son, and they will call him Immanuel'—which means, 'God with us'" (Matthew 1:23). There we are told that the great God of the universe has become "God with us" through the incarnation. It is a profound thought. But in some ways the closing thought of the book is even greater. For now we are told, not only that God was with us during the thirty-three or so years of Christ's earthly life, but that as a result of His death and resurrection He is now to be with us forever. *Now* He is with us, not just at one particular point in history or at one specific geographical location, but always and in all places equally.

There is no separation from God for those who know and are united to Christ in saving faith. What shall separate us from Christ if He has promised to be with us? Can anything? No! As Paul says, "I am convinced that neither death nor life, neither angels nor demons, neither the present nor the future, nor any powers, neither height nor depth, nor anything else in all creation, will be able to separate us from the love of God that is in Christ Jesus our Lord" (Romans 8:38-39).

If we take this command of the risen Christ seriously, two things will happen. First, we will have problems. For it is not, you understand, that we are to go to the world merely with some carefully reasoned argument for immortality. There is nothing threatening about that. The world loves that. Books that teach that—and there are many of them today—are popular. The problem is that we go rather with the proclamation of this greatest of historical facts ("Christ is risen") which, if true, demands a life-changing response from our hearers. People do not want to change, certainly not on the authority of someone else, even if that one is the Lord Jesus Christ. And not only do they not want to change, they will not, unless God first produces the most basic of all changes, regeneration, in their hearts. To go with the gospel, not of a theoretical possibility but of a Person who died and rose again and who, on the basis of that, now exercises His authority over the individual—well, that is unpopular. If it is not unpopular, it is not understood.

On the other hand, we do not have the difficulty only. We also have the promise that the all-powerful Christ will be with us to keep and bless us as we go with His gospel.

There is a fourfold repetition of the word *all* in these verses: "all authority"

(v. 18), "all nations" (v. 19), "all the commands I have given you" (v. 20), and, finally, "always," that is, "all the days" (v. 20). Problems? Yes! But as we go we have the promise that the One who speaks from the position of *all* authority, sending us to *all* the nations to teach *all* that He has taught us will be with us *always* as we present Him to the world.

OTHER BOOKS BY JAMES MONTGOMERY BOICE

Witness and Revelation in the Gospel of John
Philippians: An Expositional Commentary
The Sermon on the Mount
How to Live the Christian Life (originally, *How to Really Live It Up*)
Ordinary Men Called by God (originally, *How God Can Use Nobodies*)
The Last and Future World
The Gospel of John: An Expositional Commentary (5 volumes)
Galatians in the *Expositor's Bible Commentary*
Can You Run Away from God?
Our Sovereign God (editor)
Our Savior God: Studies on Man, Christ and the Atonement (editor)
Foundations of the Christian Faith (4-volume series):
 • *The Sovereign God* (volume 1)
 • *God the Redeemer* (volume 2)
 • *Awakening to God* (volume 3)
 • *God and History* (volume 4)
The Foundation of Biblical Authority (editor)
The Epistles of John
Does Inerrancy Matter?
Making God's Word Plain (editor)
Genesis: Creation and Fall (volume 1)
The Parables of Jesus
The Christ of Christmas
The Minor Prophets (volume 1)
Standing on the Rock

Moody Press, a ministry of the Moody Bible Institute, is designed for education, evangelization, and edification. If we may assist you in knowing more about Christ and the Christian life, please write us without obligation: Moody Press, % MLM, Chicago, Illinois 60610.